Wonder
and Other
Survival Skills

A Selection of Essays
from Orion *Magazine*

ORION

Orion Readers are published by *Orion* magazine.
All essays appeared in *Orion*.

© 2012 The Orion Society

Orion
187 Main Street, Great Barrington, Massachusetts 01230
Telephone: 888/909-6568
Fax: 413/528-0676
www.orionmagazine.org

Design by Hans Teensma/Impress

Cover photograph by Kristi Dranginis, www.kristidranginis.com

ISBN (print): 978-1-935713-02-9

ISBN (e-book): 978-1-935713-03-6

Dedicated to George K. Russell

CONTENTS

FOREWORD

THE ABILITY TO BUILD a snow cave; to can and preserve
foods; to use gunpowder to cauterize a wound; to make a
compass out of found parts; to find and cook tubers; to treat a
snakebite—these are the things we usually think of as survival
skills. But *wonder*—we don't generally think of wonder as a
survival skill. What does it have to do with weathering a crisis?
And who these days has the time or space for wonder when
we can't even fit in that canning workshop?

The din of modern life constantly pulls our attention
away from anything that is slight, or subtle, or ephemeral. We
might look briefly at a slant of light in the sky while walking
through a parking lot, but then we're on to the next thing: the
next appointment, the next flickering headline, the next task,
the next thing that has to get done before the end of the day.

But maybe it's for just that reason—how busy we are and
distracted and disconnected we are—that wonder really is a
survival skill. It might be the thing that reminds us of what
really matters, and of the greater systems that our lives are
completely dependent on. It might be the thing that helps us
build an emotional connection—an intimacy—with our sur-
roundings that, in turn, would make us want to do anything
we can to protect them. It might build our inner reserves, give

us the strength to turn outward and meet those challenges with grace.

In a day and age when we are reminded unendingly of the urgency and magnitude of the problems we face, wonder may seem like something we no longer have time for—a luxury, or a dalliance. But in one of *Orion*'s live web events, David Abram said this: "When we trivialize people's sensory attachment to the beauty of their place, to the beauty of the land wherever they live . . . we need to at least be aware that that is undermining peoples' sense of solidarity with the rest of the earth. Sensory perception is the glue that binds our separate nervous systems into the encompassing ecosystem." In other words, Abram ties our terrible, selfish decision-making about how we treat the earth—what we take from it, what we put into it, what we demand of it—directly to our estrangement from its beauty. He is saying that wonder is the antidote. That wonder is the thing that could save us.

How do we bring wonder back into our lives? How can mystery and beauty change our sense of our place in the world? How do we stay engaged in the face of darkness and uncertainty? The authors represented in this collection are playing and grappling with precisely these questions. May their words inspire us to cultivate wonder in our own lives, and to make a practice of it even in difficult times, so that we might better serve others and the places we love.

H. EMERSON BLAKE
Editor-in-Chief, *Orion*

Wonder
and Other
Survival Skills

SCOTT RUSSELL SANDERS

TELLING THE HOLY

As a boy in Ohio I lived in a neighborhood of unfinished
houses, the neighbors having run out of money or gumption
or time. Some houses rose no higher than the basement, a
dank hole in which the family huddled like bears in a cave;
others quit with a flimsy frame of two-by-fours, cloudy plastic over the windows, tar paper on the roof; still others, duly
shingled and sided, waited years for chimneys or doorknobs
or paint. There was a story of dismay or defeat behind every
halted house: fathers laid off, mothers run off, children taken
down by fever, a squall of babies, failed crops, bad bets, shoot-
ings and hauntings, whiskey, waste. Of all the stories, one
I still find troubling concerns a man who quit work on his
house because he had received what I have been listening for
all my life, a clear message from God.

Let me call the man Jeremiah Lofts. Five days a week he
worked in town at a factory that made balloons, Saturdays he
did a little scrapedirt farming on his forty acres, and Sundays
he preached in a concrete-block evangelical church. Even with
three occupations, Lofts earned precious little. For years, he
and his wife and their two, then four, and finally seven children lived in a rusting trailer on a bluff known as Ledge Hill.

They had more dogs than children, more chickens than dogs, and the entire menagerie ran loose among a confusion of sheds, lumber piles, bald tires, and junked cars.

I knew the looks of their place because I hunted fossils in the creamy limestone of Ledge Hill, and I often stopped to drink from a spring that gushed into a trough where their dirt driveway met the road. It was a public spring, safe for drinking, according to a government sign posted there. Still a believer in government signs, I would lean over the mossy lip of the trough, sipping the icy water, and study the ramshackle homestead. In daydream and nightmare, afraid of sliding into poverty, I saw myself slinking through the pack of dogs, climbing the metal stairs, and opening the crooked door of their trailer.

Then one October Saturday when the corn was in the crib, Lofts borrowed a backhoe, dug trenches, and poured footings for a proper house. Week by week that fall and winter, with help from his congregation, he raised walls and roof, ran pipes and wires, and started laying brick. In January, the cold stopped the outside work, and then in February some force greater than cold stopped the inside work. Lofts laid down his tools, quit his job at the factory, bought no seed for planting, gave up every labor except preaching. He withdrew his children from school and locked his door against the truant officer. He forbade his wife and daughters and sons to speak with anyone outside the church. He left off shaving, and his beard grew in wiry and black.

We learned what force had stopped his work on the house, what shock had jolted him out of his old life, when Lofts turned up at our front door one frozen morning, dressed in his Sunday suit, to warn us all to repent, for the world would be coming to an end on the first day of July.

"End how?" my father asked.

"By holy fire," Lofts answered. "I was praying on Ledge Hill, and the Lord spoke to me from the stars."

"Did God say why?" my mother asked.

"Because we have been wicked in our use of the earth," Lofts replied, "and the Lord means to start over with new creatures."

He did not rant. He delivered the news firmly and simply, as a man might tell his neighbors about a coming storm. Father thanked him. Mother invited him in for coffee, but Lofts refused, explaining that he had a world of people still to warn.

I was nine or ten years old, and easily spooked. I glanced from one parent to the other, trying to gauge how I should take this man's words. There was an iron conviction in his face and voice that kept my parents, and therefore me, from smiling. If God were to speak, why not to this scrapedirt farmer? Why not on Ledge Hill, where icy water poured unfailingly from the earth, where the fossils of sea creatures swam in stone? If, as newspapers and television and grown-ups declared, our long ingenious history had led only to H-bombs and race riots and war, why shouldn't the Creator begin afresh? If God were to announce a final fire, why not in the burning language of stars?

Between that February morning and the beginning of July, while Lofts delivered his warning door to door, I kept uneasy watch. Every rumor of tornadoes, every crack of lightning or grumble of thunder, every smudge of smoke on the horizon might be a token of the end.

While this great story of the world's fate played itself out, the small, everyday stories never ceased. The volunteer firemen held a pancake supper. A liquored-up father beat his kids, who limped into church all black and blue. Gas prices rose two cents a gallon. Lettuce bolted early from the heat. One of our ponies broke out of the pasture and swelled up from eating plums. The thirteen-year-old daughter of the woman who taught baton-twirling ran off with the son of the milkman. Attending to such ordinary stories in those apocalyptic days, however, was like trying to hear a drip against the roar of a waterfall.

On the eve of July first, Lofts withdrew into the shell of that half-built house to pray with his family. Whether he prayed for the world's salvation, or only for the salvation of his fellow believers, I cannot say. Whether any power heard him—whether any power capable of launching and extinguishing worlds *ever* hears a puny human voice—I do not know. I know only that the world survived, as the scoffers had insisted it would. Yet that survival seemed to me then, and seems to me now, at least as great a miracle as a dialogue with the Lord.

After the day of judgment passed without catastrophe, the prophet never showed his face in public again, not even at his church. The house was never finished. It stood for years, weeds sprouting among the unlaid bricks, tar paper curling loose from nails, paintless windows warping. Eventually the government bought the Lofts's forty acres, to be included in a park that would surround a new reservoir. One day the trailer was gone, along with the family, their chickens and dogs. A crew with bulldozer and dump trucks flattened the shabby house, hauled away every last tire and timber and brick, and sowed grass in the raw dirt. The land soon reverted to meadow, the meadow to woods.

For the rest of my time in that neighborhood, I could not pass Ledge Hill, could not sip from the spring, could not chip fossils from the limestone road cut, without remembering the prophet. Even today, dozens of years and thousands of miles later, I remain attached to that place by the thread of his story. The smell of clay and moss, the ruckus of kids and crows and dogs, the rasp of rock against my fingers, the ache of icy water on my teeth, all these and countless other details remain with me, braided together by the prophet's story.

In the same way, other narrative threads, some weak and some tough, connect me to every place I have known. Thus a river long-since dammed still runs in me, because, one winter dawn while checking muskrat traps, I slipped into the chill current and nearly drowned. A field of wildflowers blooms in me because a woman who lived there alone in a cabin once filled my palm with seeds. In memory, a forest I have not seen for twenty years still murmurs with the voice of my father naming trees, a pasture gleams under the hooves of horses, a beach dimples under the footsteps of my wife. I am bound to the earth by a web of stories, just as I am bound to the creation by the very substance and rhythms of my flesh. By keeping the stories fresh, I keep the places themselves alive in my imagination. Living in me, borne in mind, these places make up the landscape on which I stand with familiarity and pleasure, the landscape over which I walk even when my feet are still.

I have been thinking about stories of place in an effort to understand how the geography of mind adheres to the geography of earth. Each of us carries an inward map on which are inscribed, as on Renaissance charts, the seas and continents known to us. On my own map, the regions where I have lived most attentively are crowded with detail, while regions I have only glimpsed from windows or imagined from hearsay are barely sketched, and out at the frontiers of my knowledge the lines dwindle away into blankness.

There are certain spots on my map where many lines converge, like roads leading to a capitol, or like rays of energy streaming from a center of power. Ledge Hill is one such spot. I have recalled the story of the prophet because both the man and the place carry for me a tingle of the sacred. I do not claim that Jeremiah Lofts actually heard from God, only that he was listening for the profoundest speech. His business was with the ultimate ground. So is mine, however hesitant and bumbling I may be.

Traditional peoples distinguish between tales of the everyday world and tales of the spirit world, between history and myth, between profane and sacred. The distinction rests, of course, on a belief that there *is* a spirit world, an order that infuses and informs the changing surfaces we see. Visions of that sustaining realm may be sought through spiritual discipline, but they may not be summoned. If they come, they come as gifts, unforeseen. By telling stories, we conserve the memory of their passing, and we prepare ourselves for the next illumination.

I am aware of some grave objections to stories in general and to sacred stories in particular. In *Aspects of the Novel*, E. M. Forster offers an opinion that is widespread among literary sophisticates when he refers to story as "this low atavistic form." According to Forster, stories preserve "the voice of the tribal narrator, squatting in the middle of the cave, and saying one thing after another until the audience falls asleep among their offal and bones. The story is primitive, it reaches back to the origins of literature, before reading was discovered, and it appeals to what is primitive in us." Over the past century, our craving for story has provoked sighs from the likes of Henry James, Gustav Flaubert, James Joyce, Vladimir Nabokov, and Samuel Beckett. Their sighing proclaims them to be civilized, modern, free from illusion; they have left the cave to dwell outside, where stories shrivel in the harsh light of reason.

As for a belief in the sacred, that, too, according to many scholars, is a holdover from our benighted past. In *Cosmos and History*, Mircea Eliade argues that myth, ritual, taboo, every grasping for a transcendent reality, merely expresses our desire to abolish time, to resist change, to escape mortality. Nowhere is the desire to escape from the "terror of history" more nakedly revealed, according to Eliade, than in "primitive" societies. His examination of the uses of myth in ancient cultures leads him to a rhetorical question: "May we conclude from all this that, during this period, humanity was still within nature; had not yet detached itself from nature?" The moral is clear: so long as we seek an order outside of time, we remain primitive, childish, perilously close to the beasts; only by detaching ourselves from nature, weaning ourselves from sacred stories, and accepting the terror of history as the sole reality, can we become fully human.

Having read Eliade, not to mention Freud and Jung, one would be hard pressed to deny the psychological component of myth. But to go to the opposite extreme and claim that myth is *nothing but* a projection of psychic dramas is equally simplistic, and perhaps more dangerous. The danger is that in our narcissism we will be content to speak and think and care only about ourselves. Joseph Campbell avoids both extremes by arguing that myth enacts two dramas at once, that of our psyche and that of nature. In *The Hero with a Thousand Faces*, Campbell surveys the sacred stories from many ages and cultures to suggest that mythology speaks not only about the unconscious but also about the cosmos:

> *Briefly formulated, the universal doctrine teaches that all the visible structures of the world—all things and beings— are the effects of a ubiquitous power out of which they rise, which supports and fills them during the period of their manifestation, and back into which they must ultimately dissolve. This is the power known to science as energy, to the Melanesians as mana, to the Sioux Indians as wa-*

konda, *the Hindus as* shakti, *and the Christians as the*
power of God. Its manifestation in the psyche is termed,
by the psychoanalysts, libido. *And its manifestation in the*
cosmos is the structure and flux of the universe itself.

This is the belief that Barry Lopez found among hunting
peoples, that Bruce Chatwin found among the Aborigines of
Australia. You can hear it voiced by the Lakota shaman Black
Elk, by the Kiowa novelist N. Scott Momaday, by the Zen
master Thich Nhat Hanh, or by the Christian mystic Thomas
Merton. You can find it in the essays of the biologist René
Dubos, of the anthropologist Loren Eiseley, and of the physicist Freeman Dyson. You can trace it everywhere in Emerson's
work, as in "The American Scholar," where he asks, "What
is nature?" and answers, "There is never a beginning, there
is never an end, to the inexplicable continuity of this web of
God, but always circular power returning into itself." In their
various accents, these voices declare that a spiritual landscape
does indeed flicker and flame within the physical one.

I believe that this doctrine is widespread because it is
true, or at least it is as close to the truth as we have been able
to come. Sacred stories arise from our intuition that beneath
the flow of creation there is order, within change there is
permanence, within time there is eternity. Everything moves;
yet everything is shapely. The Apache word for myth means
literally "to tell the holiness." By telling the holy, sacred stories
ground a people or an individual, not merely in a landscape,
but in the power that creates and preserves the land.

If *all* of creation is holy, if one power flows everywhere—
through psyche and cyclotron, through grass and granite—
then why do we identify certain groves, mountains, or springs
as sacred? Because they concentrate our experience of the

land. We cannot hold the entire earth or even a forest or river
in our minds at once; we need smaller places to apprehend
and visit. We go to such places in thought or flesh to dream,
to renew our strength, to remind ourselves of the source of all
things; we go there as Jeremiah Lofts went to the stony crown
of Ledge Hill, to seek the power that made us.

Pilgrims often journey to the ends of the earth in search
of holy ground, only to find that they have never walked on
anything else. Here, for an eloquent example, is what Peter
Matthiessen discovered in Tibet, where he went in search of
the snow leopard and enlightenment:

> *The search may begin with a restless feeling, as if one
> were being watched. One turns in all directions and sees
> nothing. Yet one senses that there is a source for this deep
> restlessness; and the path that leads there is not a path
> to a strange place, but the path home. . . . The journey is
> hard, for the secret place where we have always been is
> overgrown with thorns and thickets of "ideas," of fears and
> defenses, prejudices and repressions.*

I have spied that secret place from time to time, usually as
through a glass darkly, but now and again with blazing clarity. One time it glowed from a red carnation, incandescent
in a florist's window. Once it shimmered in drifting pollen,
once in a sky needled with ice. I have seen it wound in a scarf
of dust around a whirling pony. I have seen it glinting from
a pebble on the slate bed of a creek. I have slipped into that
secret place while watching hawks, while staring down the
throat of a lily, while brushing my wife's hair. Metaphors are
inexact. The experience is not a glimpsing of realms beyond,
nor of becoming someone new, but of acknowledging, briefly
and utterly, who I am.

Barry Lopez, another pilgrim, has traveled from the Arctic to the Antarctic in his search for an understanding of how to live wisely within the natural order. In all his travels, he has found that wisdom embodied in stories:

> *The aspiration of aboriginal people throughout the world has been to achieve a congruent relationship with the land, to fit well in it. To achieve occasionally a state of high harmony or reverberation. The dream of this transcendent congruency included the evolution of a hunting and gathering relationship with the earth, in which a mutual regard was understood to prevail; but it also meant a conservation of the stories that bind the people into the land.*

Against those who warn us, as Forster and Eliade do, that a respect for myth and a hankering for the sacred are throwbacks to our dim origins, I appeal to the testimony of such witnesses as Lopez and Matthiessen, and to my own grounding experiences. If to be modern is to give up inquiring about my true home, then let me remain archaic. The root of *primitive*, as Gary Snyder points out, is *primus*, "or 'first,' like 'original mind,' original human society, original way of being." Sacred places, and the stories we tell about them, put us back in touch with what is original, in ourselves and in creation.

For all my conviction, the watchdog of reason inside me still raises its hackles whenever I talk about stories, and when I talk about the sacred it bares its fangs and barks. Where's the hard data? it snarls—for this is a talking watchdog, straight out of fairy tale—where's the proof? Where are the equations? the formulas? Where, oh where, are the *numbers*?

Anyone who tries to live by stories—by hearing, by reading, and especially by making them—is likely to be nagged

by the yapping of doubt. Hasn't science made myth obsolete?
Even someone as firm in her vocation as Flannery O'Connor
admitted feeling "a certain embarrassment about being a storyteller in these times when stories are considered not quite
as satisfying as statements and statements not quite as satisfying as statistics."

I very much doubt that we can live by statements, and I
am certain we cannot live by statistics. Not even scientists can
bear a steady diet of numbers. After my wife comes home
from the lab, we often talk over the day's experiments as we
are fixing dinner, and she will often say, when the results
have been confusing, that she and her colleagues haven't yet
figured out a plausible story for the data. The data themselves
only make sense, only add up to knowledge, when they are
embodied in narrative. An equation is a miniature plot: this
causes that, which causes that, which causes that.

The larger the field of explanation, the more obvious the
role of narrative. Darwin's *Origin of Species* is a story about
life on earth, and Edward O. Wilson's *Sociobiology* is a story
about human nature, and Stephen Hawking's *Brief History
of Time* is a story of the universe. Reading one account after
another, we try to make a picture of the whole by stitching
the tales together. In claiming that science is a patchwork
of stories, I am not saying it is untrue; on the contrary, I am
saying that scientists, like the rest of us, have no way of snar-
ing truth, no way of carrying it around, no way of storing it,
except in stories.

The resemblance between science and myth is most obvious at the boundaries of knowledge, where science pushes
at the limits of what can be tested by our present equipment.
Many current theories about the smallest constituents of matter, about the very early universe, about the nature of energy
and time, appear to be untestable not merely by our present

equipment but by any equipment we could conceivably build. For a physicist such as James Gunn, this is cause for lament:

> *The big problem, it seems to me, is that there is such a plethora of possible theoretical frameworks at the moment and no way of testing them. The subject is sort of running open loop. That's not very healthy from a purely scientific point of view. It's very exciting, but from the point of view of trying to learn the "truth," I think we've taken a large step backward.*

Poets and painters, novelists and musicians know only too well how it feels to choose among a plethora of frameworks. To add a single stroke, a note, a word can be an agony of decision. No gauge will tell us which of our inventions work and which ones fail. The artist swims—or drowns—in possibilities.

"The maker of a sentence," as Emerson put it grandly, "launches out into the infinite and builds a road into Chaos and old Night, and is followed by those who hear him with something of wild, creative delight." I think of my own sentences not as roads, not even as dirt tracks with a fringe of grass up the middle, but as faint, meandering paths. Comparing the scratches I have made to the infinite that surrounds me, I am reminded of Chuang Tzu's warning:

> *You are trying to sound*
> *The middle of the ocean*
> *With a six-foot pole.*

No pole will reach the bottom. No number of sentences or brush strokes or musical notes will ever exhaust old Night. Art is so tentative, so quirky, so measly compared to the universe, that only a fool would mistake it for the truth.

Many scientists, however, seem to grasp for a truth unencumbered by doubt, by mystery, a truth as plain as the hand in
front of your face. "One can take various philosophical attitudes towards the nature of the truth," the astronomer Edwin
Turner said in a recent interview,

> but if we take the most simplistic view of an external reality
> that has some truth value, and consider that our job as sci-
> entists is to try to get hold of that, I think that a hard-nosed
> rationalist might conclude that the job is too hard for us.
> There is much interesting and true stuff about the universe
> that we will never learn, or not in a foreseeable time. As I
> said, much of what we currently believe may well be wrong,
> or at least we won't be able to find out whether it's true or
> not. And I think that's very disappointing.

This will seem disappointing, this will seem a large step
backward, only if you imagine that science has *ever* given us an
unambiguous, unadorned, exhaustive picture of things. If you
believe, as I do, that science, like art, has always been a tissue
of stories—intricate, dazzling, and incomplete—then for us to
admit the limitations of our knowledge may be a step forward.

So I carve the word *mystery* on a bone and throw it to the
watchdog of reason. The dog stares at me, sniffs the bone,
then sullenly chews, lips curled, ready at any moment to rear
on its haunches and bark.

Mystery is not much in favor these days. The notion that there
are limits to what we can do, what we can know, limits to our
dominion, does not sit well with kings and queens of the hill.
Humility and reverence, we hear, are the attitudes of cowards.
Why worship a force we cannot measure on a meter? Why tell
stories about a power we cannot photograph?

Flannery O'Connor once revealed to a correspondent that her "gravest concern" was "the conflict between an attraction for the Holy and the disbelief in it that we breathe in with the air of the times." I feel that attraction for the holy, and my throat, too, burns with the air of disbelief.

When the novelist Reynolds Price published his translations of stories from the Bible in a book called *A Palpable God*, he prefaced it with a long meditation on the "Origins and Life of Narrative," in which he sought to explain why a cultivated person in our secular age might still take seriously these old tales of the holy. The "first—and final—aim of narrative," he argued, is "compulsion of belief in an ordered world." Of course it would be reassuring to believe in an ordered world, say the skeptics. But what if the universe is chaotic, a hazard of bits and pieces, and our tales of order are but soothing lullabies we sing against the darkness?

That line of reasoning leads to what I think of as the killjoy critique of sacred stories: they must be false because they are comforting. They are not, in fact, all comforting. Many are frightening. In myths, gods appear and disappear, play tricks, throw tantrums, devour the innocent and reward the wicked, bewilder the most patient seeker. The holy is often a holy terror. Still, the killjoy critique is forceful, as Reynolds Price acknowledged: "Human narrative, through all its visible length, gives emphatic signs of arising from the profoundest need of one fragile species. Sacred story is the perfect answer given by the world to the hunger of that species for true consolation." Mustn't so perfect an answer be an illusion? Not necessarily, Price added, for "the fact that we hunger has not precluded food." Water is nonetheless real for slaking our thirst, lovemaking nonetheless real for meeting our desire. I do not doubt the sun, even though it warms me and lights my way. Yes, tales about a holy power may satisfy our craving for consolation, but that proves nothing about the truth of the tales or the reality of the power.

The order we glimpse through myths is one that we did not create, that we cannot alter, that we can never fully grasp, and that we ignore at our peril. The achievements of science delude many into thinking that we have graduated from nature, that we can understand everything, that we can change or scorn conditions as we see fit, that we are the bosses of the universe. Among those who resist this delusion of omnipotence are a number of scientists. The physicist Charles Misner, for example, has articulated a humbler view:

> I do see the design of the universe as essentially a religious question. That is, one should have some kind of respect and awe for the whole business, it seems to me. It's very magnificent and shouldn't be taken for granted. In fact, I believe that is why Einstein had so little use for organized religion, although he strikes me as a basically very religious man. He must have looked at what the preachers said about God and felt that they were blaspheming. He had seen much more majesty than they had ever imagined.

By "mystery" I do not mean simply the blank places on our maps. I mean the divine source—not a void, not a darkness, but an uncapturable fullness. We are sustained by processes and powers that we can neither fathom nor do without. I speak of that ground as holy because it is ultimate, it is what makes us possible, what shapes and upholds everything we see. The stories I am most interested in hearing, reading, and telling, are those that help us imagine our lives in relation to that ground.

By telling the holy, we acknowledge that life is a gift. In fact, the whole universe is a gift. From where or what, and why, we cannot know. All we *do* know is that it issues forth, moment by moment, eon by eon, ever fresh, astounding in its richness and beauty. None of this is to gainsay the pain, the suffering, the eventual death that awaits all created things. But we measure that pain and suffering, we mourn that death, against the sheer exuberant flow of things. We can lose our life only because it has been given to us.

"The plants, rocks, fire, water, all are alive," says an Apache storyteller. "They watch us and see our needs. They see when we have nothing to protect us, and it is then that they reveal themselves and speak to us."

Oh, that things would reveal themselves and speak to us! Such was the yearning, I feel certain, that led Jeremiah Lofts to kneel on top of Ledge Hill, and led me to remember his story and his place all these years. Judging by folklore and myth, this is a perennial human desire, to converse with our neighbors in their separate dialects—to speak bear with bear, oak with oak, flint with flint—and once in a great while to leap into the universal language and hear and be heard by the Creator.

In the beginning, storytellers say, humans and animals could speak to one another, as familiarly as God spoke with Adam and Eve in the garden. The lore of many lands is filled with helpful coyotes or cats, talkative serpents or swans, wise lions, crafty crows. Even the villains—the dragons and wolves—are garrulous. Now and again a wild poet such as Blake may still converse with tigers, or a rare shaman such as Black Elk may still converse with buffaloes. But the rest of us have forgotten the universal language. Our ears have been stopped up. Our lips are sealed.

According to Hindus, God speaks Sanskrit; according to Jews, God speaks Hebrew; according to one people after another, God speaks the language of the tribe. What God speaks, I humbly submit, is the universe. Since nobody has supplied us with a cosmic dictionary, we have been laboring, word by word, over a thousand generations, to compile one for ourselves.

As I sit here this morning, sounding the ocean with my six-foot pole, my daughter Eva sits on a chair in an aviary a few miles away, observing starlings. She translates their clatter, their prancing and preening, into a code that her research team can understand. When the starlings wake before their caretakers arrive, Eva says, the birds will imitate the noise of doors opening, feet scuffling, grain being poured. That is a code even I can understand. Make the right sounds and, sure enough, the humans show up with breakfast. Our own dances and songs may be just as transparent to a mind more comprehensive than ours.

Stories about a time when we spoke easily with starlings and sycamores, with mountains and mountain goats, with our Creator in the garden, arise, I suspect, not from a memory of what was, but from a longing for what might be. Oh, that things would reveal themselves and speak to us! Why else do we teach sign language to chimpanzees? Why else do we lower microphones into the ocean to record the arias of whales? Why do we break atoms to bits and scrutinize the pieces? Why send probes into space? Why stare, through telescopes, at the wink of pulsars?

According to a theory favored by many physicists, the universe bloomed from the breaking of symmetries in the first smidgen of a second after the Big Bang. Symmetry breaking led to the preponderance of matter over antimatter, the clumping of stuff into stars and galaxies, and the division of a single force into the four we observe (gravity, electromagnetism, strong and weak nuclear forces). Myths likewise tell us that originally there was a unity, and now there is a scatter; originally there was no break between life and ground, between creatures and Creator, and now there is estrangement. When Buddhism speaks about recognizing our true Self, or Taoism about centering ourselves in the Way, or Judaism about Eden before the Fall, or Christianity about being One in Christ, they point, longingly, toward an unbroken symmetry, a primal unity.

Thomas Merton remarked on that longing in a letter to a Buddhist friend: "In any event, there is only one meeting place for all religions, and it is paradise. How nice to be there and wander about looking at the flowers. Or being the flowers." Paradise is not a place but a condition, a simple being-alive, a drinking straight from the spring. Animals seem to fill their skins, trees their bark, rivers their banks, so beautifully, that we cannot help but see in their wildness a perfect at-homeness. The words *holy* and *healthy* have the same root, which means *whole*. We perceive in nature an integrity which is our birthright, a unity in which we already participate, in which we cannot help but participate.

After admitting her embarrassment about being a storyteller in an age that preferred statements and statistics, Flannery O'Connor added that "in the long run, a people is known, not by its statements or its statistics, but by the stories it tells." By what stories shall we be known?

Within a mile or two of Ledge Hill, along the banks of the Mahoning River, I used to help a farmer named Sivvy collect buckets of sap from his grove of maples. We emptied the buckets into a barrel that rode on a sledge pulled by twin draft horses. Mr. Sivvy preferred using horses, he explained to me, because the noise of a tractor would have disturbed the trees. It would certainly have disturbed Mr. Sivvy, who spoke to the team of dappled gray Percherons with clicks of his tongue and soft words. As we worked, he told me tales about the horses, about the maples, about the river that muscled through his farm, about the clouds, the frogs, the thawing dirt. Here is what the soil needs, he told me, here is what the rains do, here is what dogwood and larkspur say about the condition of the woods. All his actions, from plowing to pruning, were informed and constrained by what he knew of his place.

Until the government built a dam and flooded Mr. Sivvy's farm, every year the maples yielded their sap without diminution, every year the soil was richer, the pastures were thicker, the birds more abundant. He lived well on his piece of earth because he was married to it by narrative as well as by nature. So might we marry ourselves to a place, commune with other creatures, make ourselves at home through stories.

We live in a land that has been known, remembered, spoken of with reverence and joy for thousands of years. Only in the last few generations has the land disappeared from our speech. In my own region of the Ohio Valley, there are few traces left of the aboriginal way. As the Shawnee, Miami, and other tribes were driven out, by arms or treaty, we lost the benefit of their long-evolved knowledge of the animals, the plants, the seasons, the soil itself. We lost nearly all of their stories and songs.

I am reminded of that loss when I read about efforts to re-establish bighorn sheep in the mountain and desert regions of the American West. Time and again, a goodly-sized herd has been released into an area where bighorns once flourished, but then, year by year, their numbers dwindle away. The problem, it turns out, is that the sheep do not know how to move between their summer range and their winter range, and so they starve. Biologists can put the sheep in ideal habitat, can rig them with radio collars, can inoculate them against disease, but cannot teach them the migration routes, which bighorns learn only from other bighorns. Once the link between sheep and ground is broken, and the memory of the trails is lost, there seems to be no way of restoring it.

We can lie to ourselves about many things; but if we lie about our relationship to the land, the land will suffer, and soon we and all other creatures that share the land will suffer. If we persist in our ignorance or dishonesty, we will die, as surely as those bighorns perish from not knowing where they are. We are smarter than sheep, in most respects. Seeing the danger of ignorance, we may be moved to invent or recover some of the lore that connects us to the land, that tells us how to live in our place.

Right now, here and there throughout America, tough-minded people are trying to reconstruct a survival lore for their own territory, their own watersheds, their own neighborhoods. I think of Robert Finch and John Hay on Cape Cod, of John Hanson Mitchell in Massachusetts, Edward Hoagland in Vermont, Wendell Berry in Kentucky, Wes Jackson in Kansas. I think of Terry Tempest Williams in Utah, Gary Nabhan in Arizona, Leslie Silko in New Mexico, Gary Snyder in California, Gretel Ehrlich in Wyoming, Ursula Le Guin in Oregon, Robert Michael Pyle in Washington, Richard Nelson and John Haines in Alaska. I think of more people than I have space to name. Whatever their training, they are all cartographers of sorts, drawing maps for particular places, giving us narratives that reveal the lay of the land, that show how the power moves, that guide us to sustenance and beauty.

In telling the holy, we do not *acquire* power, as one might gather coins in one's purse, but we acknowledge it, join with it, dwell *in* the power. The Aborigines of Australia believe that they help renew the world by recalling stories and singing songs from the beginning time. Their dreaming tracks are paths they walk and tales they tell, paths of footsteps and narrative drawn on the land. They participate in the ongoing work of nature by reaffirming the creation. "In Aboriginal be-lief," Bruce Chatwin reports, "an unsung land is a dead land: since, if the songs are forgotten, the land itself will die. To allow that to happen was the worst of all possible crimes."

As we walk our own ground, on foot or in mind, we need to be able to recite stories about hills and trees and animals, stories that root us in this place and that keep it alive. The sounds we make, the patterns we draw, the plots we trace may be as native to the land as deer trails or bird songs. The more fully we belong to our place, the more likely that our place will survive without damage. We cannot create myth from scratch, but we can recover or fashion stories that will help us to see where we are, how others have lived here, how we ourselves should live.

(1993)

BRIAN DOYLE

LOST DOG CREEK

OUR CREEK RISES at the top of a serious little hill to the west and slides all the way down our hillside into the lake below. In the summer it's a trickle and in the winter it's a bigger trickle. Only once that I remember did it get big enough to drown anything, which it did, a beaver, although I think maybe the beaver was hit by a car first, as it was not only bedraggled when we found it but much flatter than your usual beaver. My children and I were going to bury the beaver but by the time we came back with beaver-burying implements the beaver was gone. I think maybe it washed down into the lake, which feeds a massive river to the east, which feeds a massive river to the north, which feeds the Pacific Ocean, which is really massive.

No one knows what the Tualatin people who lived here called the creek, and the white people who lived here didn't write down what they called it until 1794, when the mayor, my friend Herald, had to file a resource inventory with the state of Oregon, which he did, naming unnamed or lost-named features like little creeks where beavers occasionally get drowned. Herald used to lose his dogs there so he called it Lost Dog Creek, which is its official name on maps and such now, but I have small children and they like to name things and at the moment one son calls it Squished Beaver Creek and another son calls it Found Dog Creek and my daughter calls it Not A Creek because most of the time it doesn't have any water in it.

The thing is, though, that when they ask me what I want to name the creek I don't have any words for the names I want to name it. I want to name it the way it mumbles and mutters in late fall. Or the gargly word it says after a month of rain. Or all the names of the colors it is. Or the deer-language names of the two deer we saw there once. Or the bip-bip-bip sound the deer made when they bounded away. Or the sluggish murkish sound of people dumping motor oil in it. Or a really long name like how long it's been creeking. Or the first words of all the prayers prayed there. Or the plopping sound chestnuts make when they rain into the creek every fall. Or the sound of the bamboos sucking creek water day and night like skinny green drunks. Or the whirring song of the water ouzel we saw there once. Or the wet scuttly sound of crawdads running from kids wading or the screechy sound of kids scuttling from crawdads. Or the whinnying of the million robins living there. Or the name of the first human being who ever drank from the creek. Or the proper word for the prickly pride of the old lady who lives in the moist basement of the cement house above the creek who says her husband's on vacation but he's actually been gone ten years. Or the sound that the creek doesn't make when there's no water in it. Or the sound that a kid down the street made right after she learned how to walk and she wobbled all the way down the street holding her mama's pinky and when she teetered past the creek she looked at it amazed and said an amazed word that no one has ever said before and maybe no one ever will again and the word fell tumbling end over end into the creek and away it went to the river and to the next river and to the ocean where everything goes eventually.

But I bet someday the word will come back. I bet one day a woman will be walking along the creek and when her child asks the name of the creek the mother will open her mouth and inside her will still be the kid down the street she once was and out will come the name of the creek again, salty and wet and amazed.

(2004)

DIANE ACKERMAN

WORLD AT DAWN

The pleasure of life rekindled

AT DAWN, the world rises out of darkness, slowly, sense-grain
by grain, as if from sleep. Life becomes visible once again.
"When it is dark, it seems to me as if I were dying, and I can't
think anymore," Claude Monet once lamented. "More light!"
Goethe begged from his deathbed. Dawn is the wellspring
of more light, the origin of our first to last days as we roll in
space, over 6.684 billion of us in one global petri dish, shot
through with sunlight, in our cells, in our minds, in our myriad metaphors of rebirth, in all the extensions to our senses
that we create to enlighten our days and navigate our nights.

Thanks to electricity, night doesn't last as long now, nor
is it as dark as it used to be, so it's hard to imagine the terror
of our ancestors waiting for daybreak. On starless nights, one
can feel like a loose array of limbs and purpose, and seem
smaller, limited to what one can touch. In the dark, it's hard
to tell friend from foe. Night-roaming predators may stalk us.
Reminded of all our delectable frailties, we become vulnerable
as prey. What courage it must have taken our ancestors to lie
down in darkness and become helpless, invisible, and delu-
sional for eight hours. Graceful animals stole through the for-

est shadows by night, but few people were awake to see them burst forth, in twilight or moonlight, forbidding, distorted, maybe even ghoulish or magical. Small wonder we personalized the night with demons. Eventually, people were willing to sacrifice anything—wealth, power, even children—to ransom the sun, immense with life, a one-eyed god who fed their crops, led their travels, chased the demons from their dark, rekindled their lives.

Whatever else it is, dawn is always a rebirth, a fresh start, even if familiar routines and worries charge in clamoring for attention. While waking, we veer between dreamy and lucid (from the Latin *lux*, light). Crossing that threshold each morning, we step across worlds, half a mind turned inward, the other half growing aware. "I'm still a little *groggy*," we say, the eighteenth-century word for being drunk on rum. It's a time of epic uncertainty and vulnerability, as we surface from disorienting dreams and the blindness of keeping eyes shut for many hours. As the eyelids rise to flickering light and the dimly visible, it's easy to forget where we are, even what we are. Then everything shines. Paths grow easier to see, food easier to spot, jobs easier to tackle with renewed vigor. In rising light, doors and bridges become eye-catching. We may use all our other senses in the dark, but to see we need the sun spilling over the horizon, highlighting everything and pouring a thick yellow vitamin into our eyes. We're usually too hurried to savor the elemental in our lives: the reeling sun, moon, and stars; prophecy of clouds; ruckus of birdsong; moss brightly blooming; moon shadows and dew; omens of autumn in late summer; fizzy air before a storm; wind chime of leaves; fellowship of dawn and dusk. Yet we abide by forces so old we've lost the taste of their spell. It's as survivors that we greet each day.

When the sun fades in winter, we're instinctively driven to heights of craft and ingenuity. In the Northeast, rising humans slip from their quilted night-nests and keep warm in heat gusted by fires trapped in metal boxes. Sometimes they venture out wearing a medley of other life-forms: sap from rubber trees attached to the feet; soft belly hair from Mide-astern goats wrapped around the head; pummeled cow skin fitted over the fingers; and, padding chest and torso, layers of long thick-walled plant cells that humans find indigestible but insulating and plants use to buttress their delicate tissues— that is, galoshes, wool, leather gloves, and cotton underwear. Some humans go walking, jogging, or biking—to suck more oxygen from the air—which lubricates their joints, shovels fuel into their cells, and rouses their dozy senses. Some of us migrate south like hummingbirds.

Right around Charleston, South Carolina, morning be-gins to change its mood, winter brings a chill but doesn't roll up your socks, and the sun boils over the horizon a moment sooner, because the planet's middle section begins to swell a smidgen there, just enough for pecan light at dawn, snapdrag-ons and camellias too dew-sodden to float scent, and birds tuning their pipes, right on schedule, for a chatterbox chorale.

By January, the northern bird chorus has flown to *cucaracha*-ville—or, if you prefer it anglicized, palmetto-bug-ville—where swarming insects and other lowlife feed flocks of avian visitors. There they join many of the upright apes they left behind: "snow birds" who also migrate to the land of broiling noons. We may travel far in winter, but our birds travel with us.

Painting its own time zone, its own climate, dawn is a land of petrified forests and sleeping beauties, when dry leaves, hardened by frozen dew, become ghost hands, and deer slouch through the woods, waiting for their food to defrost. Part of the great parentheses of our lives, dawn summons us to a world alive and death-defying, when the deepest arcades of life and matter beckon. Then, as if a lamp were switched on in a dark room, nature grows crisply visible, including our own nature, ghostly hands, and fine sediment of days.

(2009)

MICHAEL P. BRANCH

LADDER TO THE PLEIADES

MY DAUGHTER, Hannah Virginia, who recently turned three years old, is teaching me about the stars. Far from being a liability to her, my own profound astronomical ignorance has turned out to be her boon and, through her, a boon to me as well. The most important thing the kid has taught me is the brilliant, open secret that if you don't go outside and look up, you won't see anything. Every night before bedtime she takes my hand and insists that I get my bedraggled ass up and take her outside to look at the stars. If this sounds easy, ask yourself if you can match her record of going out *every single night* to observe the sky—something she has done without fail for more than a year now. That she has somehow brought her celestially illiterate father along is more amazing still.

Following the inexorable logic that makes a kid's universe so astonishing, Hannah insists on looking for stars no matter the weather. At first I attempted the rational, grown-up answer: "It just isn't clear enough to see anything tonight, honey." But her response, which is always the same, is so emphatic and ingenuous that it is irresistible: "Dad, we can

always *check*." And so we check. And it is when we check that
the rewards of lifting my head up and out of another long day
come into focus. One cold and windy night we stepped out
and discovered, through a momentary break in an impossibly
thick mat of clouds, a stunning view of Sirius blazing low in
the southeast. Another evening we stood in an unusual late-
winter fog and saw nothing—but then we heard the courtship
hooting of a nearby great horned owl, followed immediately
by the distant yelping of coyotes up in the hills. We even
stand out in snowstorms to stargaze, and while we've never
seen any stars on those white nights, we've seen and felt and
smelled the crisp shimmering that arrives only on the wings
of a big January storm. Snow or no snow, Hannah knows
those stars are up there, so she does easily what is somehow
difficult for many of us grown-ups: she looks for them. And
whether she sees stars or not, in seeking them every evening
she has forged an unbreakable relation with the world-within-
a-world that is night.

Questions are the waypoints along which Hannah's orbit
around things can be plotted, and she has asked so many
questions about stars for so many nights in a row that at last
I've been compelled to learn enough to answer some of them.
In doing so I've stumbled into placing myself, my family, my
home, on the cosmic map whose points of reference wheel
across the sky. We've learned a surprising number of stars and
constellations together. Now that we're in our second year of
performing our nightly ritual, we're also having the gratifying
experience of seeing our favorite summer stars, long gone in
the high-desert winter, come round again on the year's tower-
ing, dark clock.

The other evening after supper, my wife asked Hannah to
make a wish. Without hesitating she replied, "I wish I could
have a ladder tall enough to reach the stars." As usual, I didn't

know what to say. It is impossible to dismiss a three-year-old kid when she articulates hopes that are at once so perfectly reasonable and so beautifully impossible.

Before she goes to sleep, Hannah and I look at the six-dollar cardboard star wheel I bought to help us identify constellations. Too tired to make much of it, I toss the disk down on her bed in mild frustration. She picks it up, holds it upright in front of her in both hands, stares earnestly out beyond the walls of her room, and begins to turn it left and right as if it were a steering wheel.

"Where're you going?" I ask.

"Pleiades," she says. "You want to come?"

(2008)

ANN ZWINGER

THE ART OF
WANDERING

I BELONG to a tradition that traces back to Aristotle and earlier. I am a naturalist. I happen to believe that being a naturalist solves all problems and soothes all heartaches. It relieves insomnia, stops headaches and heals sundry discomforts, cures boredom, and offers an open-ended, continually expanding, fascinating exploration into distant deserts of the mind and hillsides of the heart.

In a recent interview, Miriam Rothschild, the famous British naturalist and authority on fleas, said that if she had one wish for her children it would be

> that they were interested in natural history, because I think there you get a spiritual well-being that you can get no other way, and what is more, life can never be long enough . . . I think all naturalists retain a sort of keen interest in what's going on in life. It's all part of natural history.

Naturalists are generalists. Although I admit to a predisposition toward the plant world, I am entranced by stars and starfishes, bees and bee balm, Gila monsters and gilia, mush-rooms and muskrats, and equally enthralled by a two-winged fly and a four-winged saltbush. Naturalists are the eternal col-lectors—of seed heads and seashells and empty birds' nests, of unrelated facts and myriad observations, of yesterdays and todays and tomorrows.

Naturalists find out about what goes on in the natural world through observation, which over time becomes, per-haps unconsciously, quite disciplined. Soon it is not enough just to look. One needs to identify, and then with the magic of a name in hand, begin to put together some of the facts that make up a world.

I've discovered that I observe best when I have a chance to wander. Wandering is the pursuit of happiness from east to west, bending and stooping, examining and discarding, pausing, pondering. Wandering is not going anywhere in par-ticular except just to whatever next catches your eye. All you need is world enough and time. The eminent biologist Julian Huxley wrote a marvelous book on the courtship of grebes. All that was needed for this beautifully observed and classic description of grebe behavior, he claimed, were "two weeks in the spring."

Naturalists have wandered all over the globe and all over the centuries, contributing to our knowledge of this exhilarat-ing world. Rachel Carson wandered the fringes of the sea and gave us the memorable *The Edge of the Sea*, and Nellie and Edwin Way Teale wandered their own glorious acres of Trail Wood in Connecticut, as well as the rest of the United States, and recorded the seasons thereof. Joseph Wood Krutch wan-dered the Sonoran Desert, and John Muir, the Sierra Nevada. It is no accident that naturalists are often writers: we're all prosyletizers for this best of all possible pastimes.

Wandering is, on the surface, frittering away one's time.

Within the confines of the Puritan work ethic in which I was raised, to wander from east to west, or especially from north to south, is reprehensible, quite possibly immoral, patently nonproductive, and "nice girls don't," as my mother used to say. When there are children to be jitneyed, laundry to be attended to, meals to be planned, dogs to be walked, and letters to be answered, wandering is a lily-of-the-field pursuit.

Until recently, my wandering was done somewhat surreptitiously and under many guises. Nevertheless, all these years, against philosophical and cultural conditioning, I wandered whenever I had the chance. I continue to wander because I am more than repaid with renewed productivity, fresh insights, and the joys of discovery, to say nothing of an improved disposition.

Wandering is a ticket to another level of being. It requires a modest learning how. When I became interested in wandering as a serious avocation, I betook myself to the journals of Henry David Thoreau for a lesson in wandering, or as Thoreau often called it, "rambling." For all the things for which the misfit of Concord is known, perhaps wandering is at the root of what he achieved, the most obvious as well as the most unsung facet of his life.

Thoreau developed into a wanderer; he did not start out as one, as his journals clearly show. The early journal entries tend to be sparse, brief, uneven in quality, and to me, often self-conscious. Paragraphs are short. There is no easy rapport with his reader.

In his first year of journal keeping, 1837, he compartmentalizes his observations into neat segments entitled "Bravery," "Harmony," "Crickets," "The Fog," "Heroism," and "Suspicion," pontifical titles with which a youthful writer separates himself from his reader. Passages of sharp nature observation are secondary to moralizing—in 1841 when he hears a robin singing at sunset he "cannot help contrasting the equanimity of Nature with the bustle and impatience of man."

Thoreau began living at Walden Pond in July, 1845. Almost a year later appear the first entries that indicate wandering has become an important part of his daily routine. This I understand: it takes a little while to rid oneself of all the civilized baggage one brings to one's chosen wilderness. Twenty years ago, when we first came to our place in the mountains of Colorado, I spent all my time pruning recalcitrant bushes in order to create comfortable paths. It takes time not to prune bushes.

So with Thoreau. As John Steinbeck put it in *The Sea of Cortez*, walking "is the proper pace for a naturalist. . . . We must have time to think and to look and to consider." At the end of October, 1845, Thoreau remonstrated that "you must walk like a camel, which is said to be the only beast which ruminates when it walks." That could only be written by a competent and convinced, true and dedicated wanderer. He was well aware that you cannot wander if you have to get some place on time. You cannot wander if you're in a hurry. When Thoreau was on his way to a surveying job, he was not wandering. Wandering must be done on one's own time and at one's own pace.

Thoreau well knew that solitude is another prerequisite of wandering: "By my intimacy with nature I find myself withdrawn from man. My interest in the sun and the moon, in the morning and the evening, compels me to solitude."

He wandered to all the places long known to him as a resident of Concord, and visited the same places on a rather regular basis several times a month, spicing these close-to-home wanderings with jaunts farther afield. Again he intuitively recognized another important aspect of wandering: the right place to wander. In a new place, the discoveries are so many that the mind is liable to be overwhelmed; in a place too small and familiar, the mind can become inured, or worse, clogged. The ideal is a place whose outlines you know, a place that you can visit seldom enough not to become nonseeing, but often enough to note its progressions and changes. Even then there needs to be the right spacing, the right cadence, for the mind to receive at its keenest.

As Thoreau's talents as a wanderer burgeoned, longer and longer passages of pure observation creep into his writing. His perceptions grew as his knowledge of what he was seeing grew. Likewise the length and breadth of his entries. So also the richness of his observation, as over time he awoke to an awareness of the psychology of wandering. On November 25, 1850, he wrote:

> *I feel a little alarmed when it happens that I have walked a mile into the woods bodily, without getting there in spirit. I would fain forget all my morning's occupation, my obligations to society But sometimes it happens that I cannot easily shake off the village; the thought of some work, some surveying, will run in my head, and I am not where my body is. I am out of my senses. In my walks I would return to my senses like a bird or a beast. What business have I in the woods, if I am thinking of something out of the woods?*

He acknowledges that a certain mental attitude is necessary in wandering. He notes, and rightly, the inappropriate intrusion of the outer world. In so doing, Thoreau marks the difference in states of mind between that which is active and involved in the outside world, and that state that is more contemplative and inner.

In the 1920s, brain waves were first measured and their accompanying states of mind first quantified. The variation in amplitude and frequency of brain waves can be correlated with describable psychological and physical states. During deep sleep the brain waves are slow; brain waves in a present-minded state are rapid and irregular, and are sometimes called Beta waves. Alpha waves, so-called because they were the first identified brain waves, are regularly occurring, oscillating waves indicating a state of relaxation.

The "Alpha State" is a particular manifestation of Alpha waves experienced under certain circumstances by many people. They describe a heightened awareness and sensitivity, an increased intellectual ability and alertness, accompanied by a feeling of serenity, and, often, an effortless flowing of creativity. Time expands to fit the need. This experience is highly individual but also so universal that almost everyone can recall such times of feeling "all's right with the world," when things got done by magic, when there was an infinite sense of well-being and a great sense of accomplishment that was as comfortable as it was joyous.

I suspect it's a relaxed and happy mental state in which naturalists often find themselves, and like most, I fell into it long before I knew what I was about. Those early times remain embedded like oases in landscapes of time. I remember once when I at last had the opportunity to key out a montane plant that had eluded me for months. All summer I had puzzled over it, but it was not until fall that I happened to have a plant identification book in my day pack while I was wandering.

In the mountains fall comes early and the ground was cool. All around me the wild geranium leaves were scarlet, like little red flags in the grass, reminding of the shortness of the season and the need to use well the time that was left.

As I sat beside my problem plant, it reached as high as my nose. While I explored its leaves and examined its petals, it was as if time stood still. The quiet was that of infinity. As I turned a leaf in my fingers, it was as if its chlorophyll coursed through my veins; I breathed in a green plant world and felt the warmth of the sun unfolding in my mind.

When I confirmed the identification, I felt a deep satisfaction all out of proportion to the deed. Not until I put the book down, identification made, did I feel time resume. Dragonflies clattered, grasshoppers whirred, chickadees called, violet-green swallows winnowed the lake, and I crossed back into the windy, cooling, winter-waiting world, invigorated and content. Hours might have passed for as long and as far away as I had been. By my watch it was but a few minutes.

I thought of Richard Jeffries, one of the most harmonious of English nature writers, writing a century ago, "The exceeding beauty of the earth, in her splendour of life, yields a new thought with every petal. The hours when the mind is absorbed by beauty are the only hours when we really live, so that the longer we can stay among these things so much the more is snatched from inevitable Time."

Sometimes there is a wish to record moments such as these, to preserve them in writing; as Edwin Way Teale said, to preserve a moment and place in time in the same intricate detail that a fly is preserved in amber. If so, there's a problem. One thing one generally does *not* do when wandering is to record at the moment, for the physical act of note-taking disrupts concentration and focus. On-the-spot note-taking pulls and tugs me into another frame of mind, which I would acknowledge as Beta, a busy, present awareness of pencil marks on paper that can be the antithesis of the otherworldly Alpha state of wandering.

The only solution is to wait and record everything as best one can remember when paper and pencil and tabletop are available; to re-walk mentally the hours and footsteps on the paths of the day, to allow the mind to recreate and recrystallize, to evaluate and collate, to process vagaries of time and place into a glistening coherent whole. Even Thoreau, with his well-disciplined mind, couldn't call back everything in sequence, and "I forgot to say . . ." and "I forgot to mention . . ." pepper his entries, as if he were stumbling over the wealth of his own words.

For a writer, quite obviously the Alpha state is a highly profitable state to enter at times of one's own choosing. With training and self-discipline, similar to deep relaxation techniques, it can be entered at will. I am convinced that Thoreau was able to write so tellingly because he made a practice of wandering and, while wandering, entered into an Alpha state that enabled him to perceive and describe with extraordinary clarity. In other words, when Thoreau hit his stride as a wanderer, he also hit his stride as a writer. He understood early on the psychological beneficence that came from wandering, that when his eye was busy, his mind was free to play with new connections and perceptions. In wandering he fully entered the natural world and enhanced his development as a writer.

Fortunately, one doesn't need to be a writer to wander. A withdrawal from man's society into that of nature's is our great safety valve (and also one of the most immediate reasons for retaining our wildernesses, great and small). The benefits of wandering are there for anyone who makes the time and cares to develop an observant eye.

Wandering doesn't even have to be shank's mare. Horizons can expand just with the looking. Last April, in a rather dour frame of mind, I stood overlooking our pond in the Colorado mountains, watching the cloud reflections come in from the west. The morning sun was still low. It warmed one side of my face while the wind bit the other.

A soft whistling of wings came through the wind's humming. Two mallards wheeled around the shore, turned upwind, descended, skittered a long trail across the surface of the cool morning pond, and plopped down softly for a landing.

I watched for a moment as they arranged the water around them to their liking, then I went inside to mark their arrival on a bird list I keep on the back of the closet door—the list of all the birds common to 8,300 feet in Colorado is not a very long one. Listed there are the resident chickadees and grayheaded juncos, Stellar jays and white-breasted nuthatches. There are the foragers who come by weather rhythms—white-headed juncos warning of coming snow and brown-capped rosy finches blown down by tundra storms. Some define the seasons, as the nighthawks who mark the return of summer and the kingfisher who rattles warning at every minnow within hearing in the spring.

I lifted the pages beneath, each page a previous year. On each, the mark matches: the mallards have always arrived the second week of April. In the coolness of the morning I felt a wonderful flush of pleasure. They came back, just as the chart said they should, as if, because they'd been marked down, they were duty-bound to appear, as if pencil symbol on paper called them to this necessity.

Ridiculous thought, but it persisted. I believe in the magic of lists. Lists order my otherwise exceedingly untidy life. The naturalist in me keeps phenologic lists of what goes on in the natural world and when. Born of the necessity to know when to plant and when to harvest, phenology endures because it satisfies a human need to connect, to anticipate and to enfold, to expect and to recognize, to understand.

You can't keep phenological charts of your children. Next year at this time they will not return to this same pond—the essence of childhood is growth and unpredictability. Only in

Peter Pan does Wendy come back every spring. Nor can you keep a phenology of your own life. We may be creatures of habit, but the advent of the unexpected is more sure than continuing status quo. In this world of change and infinite possibilities, *I liked* seeing the mallards return to their pond. Their arrival wove up the tag ends of this mountain spring, which had frayed itself out over hopeless cold months; it reestablished a necessary rhythm.

They come, unerringly (or so it seems to me) to this small pond. If not the original pair, then their offspring, bonded to this pond and this place in the same way as I. The second week in April. They keep no calendars, no lists. They operate with more subtle and lasting instincts than those with which I am equipped. Yet I am given the sentient pencil to record their return and they stabilize my spring.

The wind cut sharp, shirred the surface, and the ducks lifted off. I knew, for a moment, the buoyancy of water. The wind flowed under my wing feathers, and the treetops spun away beneath me even as my feet remained on the wooden plank deck. I watched them until they disappeared against a lowering sky, inordinately pleased and reassured, knowing they would return. Only minutes had passed, yet I had glimpsed unknown distant waters, skimmed over cattails, and stirred up duckweeds. I came back to this chill world refreshed and cheerful. The ducks were here where they belonged. I was here where I belonged.

Wandering allows you to step into another frame of mind as easily as slipping on an old, comfortable jacket, to step out of a human-centered world into one in which you are only another piece of a larger puzzle. Indeed, one of the ways of stepping into an Alpha state is to use a physical device, to program yourself so to speak, so that when you slide your arm into that familiar jacket you slide into a wandering frame of mind.

I learned something important about wandering when the jacket I had worn for years was stolen—why I cannot imagine. It was scarcely the garment dreams are made of. It was past almost everything. The down was past providing much serious warmth but it was just the right loft to bundle up for a pillow when backpacking. The zipper had long since refused to function and the windflap snaps were showing a rebellious tendency to pull out of the nylon. The front was shiny with the smoke of many campfires and the fabric had come to exude that unmistakable brittle odor. But it wrapped around my shoulders like affection and my hands fitted into its pockets like peace.

When it was gone I had to break in a new one. I dreaded it, fearing that I had lost a passport to another country where I also lived. I was afraid that that old jacket took with it, along with an old stub of pencil and a scrap of defunct grocery list, my easy slippage into a wandering frame of mind and a fold of my serenity.

It's taken time to realize that the old jacket, much as I loved it, was only a device, and that the only ticket necessary to wandering was there for the asking. It was in my head. So I wander without my old jacket but with a new realization that one wanders the furrows of the mind as well as the marvels of the fields, and that wandering is as much in the slant of attitude as in the slant of metatarsal.

In wandering there is great reassurance, for it is then one fits into the continuum of a larger world, a world which for the naturalist has no beginning and no end. We all need to know that there is purpose and worth and reason in living. A naturalist finds these in the sibilant logic of saltating sand grains spinning into a dune, in the spoked spine patterns of a cactus and the hexagonal mud cracks in a dry arroyo, in bee-beset willow catkins and in clouds that curtain a western summer sky with virga.

Naturalists wander and wonder: they observe and collate, mark the seasons and their symptoms. They deal with the world as a unity. When one follows a solitary bumblebee working a penstemon, wonders why the petals are blue and the buds are pink, asks the question and receives with the answer a whole bouquet of new questions, when one finds out why there was a yesterday and sits by a river and listens to what makes a tomorrow, one finds a world that makes sense, that is infinitely reasonable, and works superbly well in a way that our peopled, everyday world frequently does not.

We need logic and structure, we need to be reassured that this is, after all, a rational world. It's a thin reassurance if one bases it upon the actions of the human species. People don't always perform rationally; nature does. The sun always rises in the east. There is a reasonable confidence that it will do so tomorrow without asking for a revision of its working hours.

For a naturalist, there is always something to see or touch or smell or taste or hear: orange jewel lichen scabbed on the rough dark rocks of a lava flow; a desert lily trumpeting in the spring; the sinus-clearing smell of sagebrush or the wind breathing the ephemeral sweetness of an evening primrose at dusk; the tartness of an *Oxalis* leaf or the sweet nectar in an Indian paintbrush; spadefoot toads trilling a message of warmth and water and the virtues of tadpoles. The stability and reason of the natural world are star cones of light intersecting across an infinity of sky.

Naturalists listen to the ticking of water in plant veins: there are *good* things going on in there, in leaf vein and heartwood. Therein lies sanity, security, and serenity—especially for this naturalist, who loves frogs and fritillaries, river rocks

and liverworts, mosses and moonbeams, dawns and dobson-
flies, and drifts of wild white anemones blowing along a
mountain stream, and whose fortune cookie slip just read:
"Nature, time, and patience are the three best physicians."

(1986)

ALERIA JENSEN

GATHERING INDIGO

I KNEEL IN THE MUSKEG, bucket between my legs, cushion of sphagnum moss crimson beneath my rubber boots. My fingers follow an old pattern: pluck, twist, plop into the bucket. Among the browning skunk cabbage beneath the jack pines, clusters of bunchberry announce fall's arrival like splashes of wine. Nearby my brother leans into the hillside.

I have picked blueberries on this island for as long as I can remember. Before me—mother, father, grandmother. A hundred years, and every year the berries bring their summer glow to our freezers, our ovens, our plates.

The search image for berries lies deep in my body, wherever such inclinations reside. Scan the meadow, the forest edge, the avalanche chutes. Highbush or lowbush? Blueberry or black huckleberry? Wrinkled and wormy or a plump, perfect, purple sphere? My eyes don't even pause on the empty bushes. Scan left, right. Up ahead—jackpot. A loaded bush, heavy with fruit. Bend over, pick till your back hurts. Fall to your knees, pick. Stretch. Sink back down. The harvest is deeply satisfying, an old rhythm of provisioning for winter, of sharing in what the land has to offer. I am slowed into meditations on the shape of leaves, the rising scent of earth, the gradual cycle of ripening.

This is one of the great traditions of my life.

Today, half the berries I touch dissolve beneath my fingers, the waterlogged spheres spitting soggy grains from their skins. This has been southeast Alaska's wettest summer in thirty years. Many of us in the rainy capital city have spent a good deal of time and conversation feeling sorry for ourselves, owing to the particular lack of sunshine this year. And now fall has come, light is waning, water has gotten to the berries. Grumbling, I mutter to my brother about the sodden mush I keep picking. He replies, "The land just gives and gives and gives, and all we do is show up." Looking up from a bush, he adds, "I think they're in exceptional condition, given everything they've been through."

I continue to pick and realize he is right. *All we do is show up.* Wake up, drink our coffee, jump in the car, head for these boggy slopes. Expect the land to provide. And it does. Despite the soggy ones, there are plenty of good berries. Plenty for us, for bears and birds and insect larvae. Plenty for muffins, pancakes, and smoothies. Even if it takes longer to fill our buckets, if some fruits are saturated, if we slip and slide and have to hold our pails high above the dripping branches. It's part of living among wilderness, in a rainforest. Part of why we love it here.

I find myself feeling a huge gratitude, not only for what the land shares, but what it endures. *Given everything they've been through.* Mid-September, cold mists, no sun by which to ripen, berries still hanging on. I think about the story line leading to each fruit. The poor drainage and low nutrients that give rise to the muskeg. The perennial ericaceous shrub surviving winter temperatures and darkness. The pink blossom opening in April or May. The dusting of pollen that must be exchanged, the hovering of bumblebees and hummingbirds. Each fruit an evolution.

At the end of the day, covered in mud, tongues purple, we tramp down through fog and reddening moss. We stop to pop berries into our mouths, last tastes for the day. These tart ones, so different from the sweet domesticated ones sold by the pint at the supermarket. Within it, each fruit holds what I hold: an accumulation of place. The tangy explosion of these northern berries on the tongue is the landscape communicating itself, an expression of its essential wild character. *Taste me—here is your peat moss, your snowmelt, your glacial till. Here is your hemlock root, your jack pine, your overwintering bee. Taste me.*

(2007)

RICK BASS

THE RETURN

Symmetry and other springtime delights

ALL THROUGH THE WINTER, the deer have traveled the
same paths over and over, packing the deep snow, their sharp
hoofs downcutting to form lanes, and then nearly tunnels,
through the soft drifts. They keep these trails so packed down
that the snow in them gets compressed into some kind of
super-dense, cobalt- or galena-colored substance, more slippery than mercury, more dense than lead—and paradoxically,
or so it seems at first, these trails, which once marked where
the snow had been worn down to its thinnest margins, are
now the last remaining threads of winter: fifteen feet of snow
supercompressed to a height of only a few inches, so that even
in the returning warmth of May, these luminous ice trails lin-
ger long after all the snow has melted; and having no need to
use these trails, which are slippery now, the deer avoid them.
Instead, the deer step carefully across the spongy dark duff—
surely they must feel spritely, unencumbered, at long last—
and in this yin-and-yang inversion, white snow to black earth,
they shed their winter coats, leaving their hollow hair in tufts
and clumps all over the woods, the braided, winding rivers of it
running now at cross-angles to the old paths of hoof-matted ice.

The hair glints in the newer, sharper light of springtime, looking like spilled straw, or silver needles—trails of it leading all through the woods—and this shift in the riverine sentences that echo the deer's passages—a shift even more pronounced than the reversal of a tide—is for me, as with the coming of the first trillium, one of the most visual markers of the season, the true and irreconcilable end of winter. Though the mud and forest puddles will dry out, and the winds will soon enough scatter those concentrated rivers of hair to a more democratic and widespread distribution, in May it is still all clumps and patches, the deer shedding great wads of hair against any rough surface: the bark of a hemlock, the stub of branch on a fallen lodgepole. And all throughout the forest, too, are the whitened, ribby spars of winter-killed deer, appearing like so many ships stranded by the white tide's great withdrawal; and in caves and hollows too, beneath the fronds of great cedar trees, entire mattress nests of deer hair can be found where a mountain lion has fed all winter long: dragging one deer after another to his or her favorite cache and gnawing on them until the bones stack upon one another like a little corral and the disintegrating hides shed their fur. After the end of winter, in such places, the ground may be half a foot deep in white belly hair—the snow-tide pulling back from the lion's lair, retreating horizontally, with new life poised at the leaping edge of vertical green roar . . .

May is a wonderful time to see the eagles, both bald and golden, the former returning with the opening of the river ice; and during this period they feast gluttonously on the moraine of an entire winter's worth of road-killed deer. Nearly every morning on the drive to school in early May my daughters, Mary Katherine and Lowry, and I will pass at least one such eagle banquet, with two or three bald eagles—both the mature adults and the adolescents, which are just as large but don't yet have the white head—accompanied often by a golden eagle or two, and when the eagles see a car or truck approaching, they abandon their roadside feast and on great wide wings flap, wheeling in all directions to their various sentinel perches like children who had been roughhousing while their teacher stepped away from the classroom scrambling back to their seats upon whispered news of the teacher's return. Fur from the deer carcasses loosened by the eagles' talons swirls in the air, glinting like pins and needles, deer hair stirred on the currents of the eagles' departure and by the passage of our truck.

Time and time again I am astounded by the regularity and repetition of form in this valley and elsewhere in wild nature: basic patterns, sculpted by time and the land, appearing everywhere I look. The twisted branches in the forest that look so much like the forked antlers of the deer and elk. The way the glacier-polished hillside boulders look like the muscular, rounded bodies of the animals—deer, bear—that pass among those boulders like living ghosts. The way the swirling deer hair is the exact shape and size of the larch and pine needles the deer hair lies upon once it is torn loose from the carcass and comes to rest on the forest floor. As if everything up here is leaning in the same direction, shaped by the same hands, or the same mind: not always agreeing or in harmony, but attentive always to the same rules of logic; and in the playing-out, again and again, of the infinite variations of specificity arising from that one shaping system of logic an incredible sense of community develops—a kind of unconscious community, rarely noticed, if at all, but deeply felt.

Felt at night when you stand beneath the stars and see the shapes and designs of bears and hunters in the sky; felt deep in the cathedral of an old forest, when you stare up at the tops of the swaying giants; felt when you take off your boots and socks and wade across the river, sensing each polished, mossy river stone with your cold bare feet. Felt when you stand at the edge of the marsh and listen to the choral uproar of the frogs, and surrender to their shouting, and allow yourself, too, like those pine needles and that deer hair, like those branches and those antlers, to be remade, refashioned into the shape and the pattern and the rhythm of the land. Surrounded, and then embraced, by a logic so much more powerful and overarching than anything that a man or woman could create or even imagine that all you can do is marvel and laugh at it, and feel compelled to give, in one form or another, thanks and celebration for it, without even really knowing why . . .

Each morning in May I feast hungrily on the sight of the eagles pulling loose with their beaks and talons the tufts of deer hair that are so much like the shape of the larch and pine needles upon which the carcass rests, and into which the remnants of the carcass will soon be dissolving, the trees and bushes then growing up out of that deer-enriched soil to sprout branches that are the same shape as the antlers had been. One story. Many parts, but only one story, and the rhythm of each month carrying us along, beneath, or within that one chorus.

It seems extraordinary to me to see such a sight on the way to school nearly every morning, in the awakening days of May, and I like to consider how such images—in both their singular beauty as well as in the braided rhythm that is created by their accumulation—help to comprise the fabric of the girls' childhood, days of wild green regularity so incomparable to and unquestioned by any other experience that such sights seem "normal" to them, though even in the dailiness of it, the wonder of May, and of all the months here, I try to explain to the girls to not take such things for granted—saying this even as I am fully aware that there is a part of me that most wants them to take such sights for granted; to accept such bounty as their unquestioned due, to perceive it as regular and familiar—and no less beautiful in that familiarity.

In a way that I haven't yet figured out how to fully articulate, I believe that children who get to see bald eagles, coyotes, deer, moose, grouse, and other similar sights each morning will have a certain kind of matrix or fabric or foundation of childhood, the nature and quality of which will be increasingly rare and valuable as time goes on, and which will be cherished into adulthood, as well as becoming—and this is a leap of faith by me—a source of strength and knowledge to them somehow. That the daily witnessing of the natural wonders is a kind of education of logic and assurance that cannot be duplicated by any other means, or in other places: unique, and significant, and, by God, still somehow relevant, even now, in the twenty-first century.

For as long as possible, I want my girls to keep believing that beauty, though not quite commonplace and never to pass unobserved or unappreciated, is nonetheless easily witnessed on any day, in any given moment, around any forthcoming bend. And that the wild world still has a lovely order and pattern and logic, even in the shouting, disorderly chaos of breaking-apart May and reassembling May. That if there can be a logic and order even in May, then there can be in all seasons and all things.

(2009)

DAVID GESSNER

WHEN YOU SEE A SKIMMER

I DARE YOU not to get excited when you see black skimmers scything along the shoreline. I dare you to stay in your own mumbling head, running around on the same hamster wheel of thought. I dare you, as they mow the water, scooping up tiny fish with their preposterous bills, to not at least momentarily skip out of self.

Of course I know you *can* resist. Skimmers are not the only miraculous animals after all, and human beings excel, beyond all else, at becoming absorbed in their own self stories. But if you actually turn away from those stories and look at these birds for a moment, really *look*, you'll need to pause and briefly rearrange the way you think about the world.

Here's what you'll see:

A line of birds flying along the shore, the size of small gulls but unmistakably not gulls. Maybe they're terns, you think for a second, but like no terns you've ever seen. An electric red-orange shines from the bills before abruptly turning to black halfway toward the tip. It's a candy-corn color, a color from the pages of a comic book, certainly not something you'd

expect to find on real birds. But they *are* real, and the only
birds that have a lower mandible longer than the upper, the
better for scooping. They patrol the shore, jaws dropped (like
yours maybe), grazing the water and hoping for accidental
contact with a fish. At the merest touch, a built-in tactile trig-
ger in their jaw sends a signal to their upper bill, the maxilla,
which instantaneously snaps shut.

This might sound miraculous, a thing of wonder, but of
course to the fish it is a different, not so wonder-full, story.
To the fish the skimmer's oversized lower mandible cutting
through the water might as well be the reaper's scythe. But
you won't worry too much about the fish as you watch the
bird fly belly to belly with the ocean, so close that its reflection
seems to fly below it through the water. Instead you'll watch
that lower mandible, the very front part, kick up its small
wake as it plows forward. You'll notice that the birds actually
leave a line behind them in the water.

Curious, maybe, you'll turn to books. You'll learn that
skimmers were once called "sea dogs" for the strange, garbled
barking sounds they make. You'll learn that, like us, they are
creatures of edges, harvesting the edge of water and land,
working the edges between day and night. Your field guide
will wax poetic about their "buoyant" flight, about how they
execute "hairpin turns and smooth banks while foraging,"
how "their flocks wheel in unison." As you read on, it may
occur to you that evolutionists and creationists could fight for
hours over this bird. Days, maybe. Who, after all, the latter
group would argue, but a creator, and a creator with a sense
of humor, could have created *this*? The joke-shop nose, the
funny barking, the crazy way of getting dinner. The former
group would rebut that the silly bill is fit exactly to its task, so
could have evolved into no other shape. The only thing the
two camps will agree on, throwing up their hands, will be the

bizarre uselessness of the bill's candy-corn color.

You, however, will become greedy for skimmers. You'll start planning your walks for dawn or dusk so that you can see them gracefully mowing the water. Of course to say that you will return from your walks changed is an exaggeration. Maybe you'll barely remember the sights of the scything birds during the rest of your day. But if not fundamentally changed, you will be in some unspoken way mildly altered. At the very least you'll have experienced a blip in the day's habitual worry. Perhaps, better yet, those sharp bills will have given you a cutting gift, slicing through the nettles of thought long enough for you to notice briefly that there are vast worlds beyond your own.

(2007)

SUSANNE ANTONETTA

GODS AT PLAY

MY SON and his friend David run a day-care center. The boys
started the day care in their schoolyard, and though my Jin's
only seven, he heads a small staff, all of them moss- and
muck-bottomed, nails brackish-green. They squat and hover,
prodding their wriggling charges—a nest of roly-polies—into
place. They also supervise the day care's teachers, a pair of
earthworms. Legless, bloodless, and slow, the worms are at
a disadvantage where the kids place them, at the head of the
roly-poly tumble.

Most properly called pill bugs, though sometimes known
as potato bugs or potato beetles or even woodlice, roly-polies
look like mini-armadillos (Latin name *Armadillidium vul-
gare*—common little armadillo). Touched, they curl up into
armored balls, round bullets. They're not beetles, nor are
they insects, or even arachnids; they're crustaceans, sharing
an ancestor with lobsters and shrimp. Of course, none of the
children think of them as little land-lobsters when they twig
them back into their moss enclosure. Bugs are bugs.

The day care lies at the base of an oak tree, in the damp
organic matter pill bugs love. Like earthworms, pill bugs are
natural composters, eating what falls to the ground. But the

earthworm teachers, mulchers by trade, show no talent for caretaking: their charges crawl right off on their seven pairs of legs. The children scoop them back and tuck them under leaves. The pill bugs disappear between recesses anyway, and have to be replenished.

I arrive one day to pick Jin up and find the kids hunched together at the tree, Jin's straight black hair next to David's blond ruckus of curls. "Not yet," he murmurs, speaking I suppose to my shadow, as I haven't said anything so far. "Not yet." The fingers of a seven year old aren't much longer than the cap of a pen, and they still have a just-learning fumble—the boys' faces shrink with concentration as they grasp a roly-poly, pile up useless barriers of leaves. Jin continues to murmur, seeming barely to hear himself. "You, go back, you're not supposed to go that far," he scolds a wayward bit of leggy crustacean.

"As flies to wanton boys are we to the gods," Gloucester says in *King Lear*. "They kill us for their sport." I remember my coiffed aunts mouthing, "Boys will be boys," mildly approvingly, at whatever frog/beetle/jellyfish boy-mayhem happened to go on. What would Gloucester—or my aunts— think of these boys, who even consider the roly-polies' need for amusement? There's the Dunk-O-Twig, which can drop a small object to the ground if hit correctly with a pebble. Little ponds built into the day-care grounds. Oak leaves scraped up into beds for napping.

In handouts on pill bugs, state extension services stress their harmlessness; they don't damage wood and rarely eat fresh plants, preferring decay. Nevertheless, these services give elaborate instructions for killing them—with Sevin, Dursban, Diazinon, many of these chemicals developed for human warfare. It's a given that we'd want to kill them; there are lots of them, after all, often found piling together under bricks or flagstones. Such volume in the insect world offends our human sensibilities.

But not at seven. At seven, at least some of us coax the pill bugs into order, and admire the plated, squirming piles we'll someday, presumably, find vulgar. I want to say we're born tender; I know we probably have both possibilities inside us— the hand that ministers, the hand that dismembers. I believe my Jin is tender; I know sometimes he isn't. He may be a wanton boy. But as models for the gods go, his fingers closing with willed softness around the pill bug's shell, I would take him. I would take him any day of the week.

(2006)

AMY LEACH

PEA MADNESS

Of tendril-wending, chance-taking, and desire

IF YOU HAVE ONLY ONE MIND, or one stewpot, you will be
forced to entertain a hodgepodge. Many of the pre-Vikings
only had one pot, so they ate their peas as part of a hodgepodge called Ärtsoppa, with millet and sesame and panic and
poppy. Ärtsoppa upgraded the pea—*any* fellow ingredients
would have upgraded that ancient pea, musty and cartilagi-
nous, good for filling silos or baby rattles.

By the 1600s, however, peas had become dear, like delft-
ware. Many Holland seedsmen, now involved in obscurity,
were once involved in the quality of the pea. They rendered
the rattle-pea succulent and creamy. Peas were not just avert-
ers of hunger anymore: pea-eating was a madness. Fresh tender green peas were escaped from dances for, stolen at midnight from kitchen larders, smuggled by pocket into church,
considered one of the very merits of life, often so hardtack.

At first the life of the *Pisum sativum* does not seem to be
that of a mad-maker. The young pea plant lives by diligent
routine, forming two tiny, equal leaves every four and a half
days. If leaf-leaf on Tuesday morning, then leaf-leaf on Saturday evening, and leaf-leaf on Thursday morning. Someone

who helps peas—a friar or a bee—may look in on them, but young peas are as autonomous as mushrooms and responsible as clocks.

But then, what had seemed a mushroomlike spirit of autonomy turns out to be just the delusive stability of shortness. Peas are clocky children who become spoony adults. Once they grow long-limbed, they start to teeter, because they possess more self than they can support. Then they grow madly wending tendrils, to sweep the air for lattices—just as teetery marionettes will grow marionette cords to sweep the air for marionetteers. Yearning begets yearning: the pea plant yearns for a lattice, so it grows tendrils—then every tendril too yearns for a lattice. Yearning draws tendrils out of the spindly green pea-shoot only to find itself compounded, elephantine.

Tendril wending is swervy and conjectural; like a dancer who cannot hear the music, pea tendrils are antic with inapprehension. Since there is no way for them to apprehend a lattice, the only direction to grow is yonder. Haywire personalities, like peas, wobbly personalities with loose ends, iffy ends, result not from having no aim, no object in life, but from having an *extrasensory* object. What they want is beyond their powers of apprehension—until they hold it in their acute green wisps—so their manner is vagabond. The personality that longs only for perceptible things is down-to-earth, like a dung-eater. But the teetery-pea kind send out aerial filaments to hound the yonder, tending every which way, guessing themselves into arabesques, for they are fixed on the imperceptible.

The truth is that lattices are not the only things that are extrasensory. When you cast your small questioning arms into the opaque universe, you may find a trellis to tether yourself to; or you may find a tree sticky with birdlime; or a snuffling piglet; or a trapeze artist swinging by who takes you for an aerialist and collects you—then alas, unless you have excellent timing and a leotard, you will be a lost cause.

Or you might find nothing, in which case your yearning will unhorse you. Yearning can horse you or unhorse you. You can only look for so long before your looking apparatus topples you over. Maybe there is no lattice within your reach, for not every plant is issued a lattice, just as not every planet is issued a people and not every person a pudding and not every pudding a plum. Or there may be a lattice right there next to you, installed with you in mind, around which your feelers verge and twist but never touch until finally, freighted with longing, you fold, same as the plant with nothing nearby. The lattice an inch away might be a moon, a myth, an abstraction. You might have grown your tendrils as filigree.

If the road from pea to pea is shortened, the plants can be lattices for each other, like marionettes winding their cords around one another—*hold me up, Blue Baroque Lady; hold on to me, Lindenwood Gnome*. But then the pea patch becomes a pea ward, because "mildew cometh by closeness of air." Crowds do not divide the blight but multiply it. On May Day everybody dances around the Maypole together and everybody feasts together and the plague travels from him to her to him to him. More people means more plague, more wood means more fire, more peas means more mildew. Pea powdery mildew will infect the pea and the pea and the pea, not just the pea.

Pea powdery mildew spores travel by being puffed around by the wind—they might get blown into a community swimming pool, or a henhouse, or onto a freshly painted mural. In fact, anything but a pea plant is a cemetery for them; though sometimes they land nowhere and remain in the air, unberthed with the specters. Once in a while a flurry of spores gets blown straight into the thin, seeking arms of a *Pisum sativum* plant. Then the spores settle down and with their hollow haustoria grieve the plant; they drink its terminable green blood, making it powdery-pale and curly-weak; but they drink carefully, sipping slowly through their straws, for how can you drink from an empty glass? If in all this wide herby world, if in all this gardeny world of Moonflowers and Lespedezas and Daphnes and Daisies and Frangipanis and Ghostweed and Bluets and Galaxes and Blazing Stars and Blood-on-the-snow and Mind-your-own-business and Porcelain Berries and Rain Lilies and Chinquapins and Withywinds and Salsifies and Fritillaria, you light on the one thing you can live on—Pea Plant—why would you drain it dry and give yourself back over to the air? The air is a question and those who travel upon it travel in questions: When will I find what? Where is who?

Long ago, long before the air and its travelers, there was an immense void between Muspelheim and Niflheim, the lands of fire and ice. It was called the Ginnungagap—the gaping gap, dark and empty. But when the Fire Giants from Mus-pelheim trooped across the Ginnungagap to war with the Frost Giants from Niflheim, there was provoked some lively melting, and the yeasty droplets flung into the void became persons and plants and beasts. These proliferated and filled up the emptiness; and for the ones who can easily reach the materials they need, the Earth is nothing like a gap; they are content, like clocks endlessly fingering integers.

But there are others who still experience the Ginnunga-gap. Into the gaping gap Buttercups send their yellow-dusted anthers, petitioning for a bee; into the gap the Crane Flower sends its blue landing-petals and orange flicker-flame petals, to doubly tempt the Sunbirds with blue stability and orange witchery. Into the gap the *Pisum sativum* dispatches its loopy tendrils. But like a lost wolf howling for her pack, whose long strains of *find me* might attract the wrong wolves, the plants might summon the wrong thing with their susceptible anthers and petals and tendrils. Instead of Sunbirds, landing-petals might receive Diseases that cause corkiness, mushi-ness, yellowness, sogginess, stinkiness, and spots.

Why even take the chance? Why try at all? Why not stay safe in the dirt, a seed holding tight, instead of a seed bursting forth and offering the plummy stationary self to slime mold and powdery scab and blossom-end rot and weevils and sow bugs and gangrene and silver scurf and scrappy little sparrows waiting above ground?

Plants cannot stay safe. Desire for light spools grass out of the ground; desire for a visitor spools red ruffles out of twigs. Desire makes plants very brave, so they can find what they desire; and very tender, so they can feel what they find. Thus Genips with hearts of honey-pulp; thus Poppies with hearts of fringe, and Pickerelweeds with hearts of soft pale purple frill, and Tulips with tilting hearts, and Foxgloves with downy freckled hearts, and the maddeningly sweet hearts of the careening pea. Those who are feeling their way into the gaping gap must be able to feel, which means able to freckle, and fringe, and soften, and tilt. And if they can tilt they can fall—which is a different design from that of the ticking hearts of crystal-quartz.

(2010)

CHRIS DOMBROWSKI

KANA

A father grasps at the nature of wonder

TO REACH THE HONEY HOLE I have to cross a channel of knee-high, silt-stained river with twenty-month-old Luka, my mushroom-picking partner, on my shoulders. I wade in: the soles of my sandals clambering for purchase on the moss-covered cobbles, the cold flow kiting my pant legs, Luka's knees tightening around my neck. Ashore, cuffs draining, I tell the boy, "We'll beeline it for the old burn," where

I sense the freshest morels are poking out in droves from the undergrowth. But ten yards into our beeline, I'm crouching to pluck a three-inch-tall yellow morel from a patch of Solomon's seal, then two, thimble-sized, from the dappled shade of a ratty cottonwood.

A red-shafted flicker's call slits the quiet of the wet May woods.

"Wha's that?" Luka asks.

"That's a flicker," I say, mimicking its call with a whistle.

"Flicka," he says, then tests the air with his own scream-like rendition.

The bird responds to neither.

Shifting, squirming on his perch, the boy wants down. I

let him off, my shoulder muscles uncrimping—then spot a small gathering of the honeycombed, conical caps on a south-facing ditch bank, a little board meeting of morels. "Look, Bud—mushrooms!" I say, nearly diving to slice my stationary quarry off at the stem. "And how about this one?" I'm marveling at a hand-tall specimen. None too impressed, Luka stares into the budding branches, their wide grasp of sky.

It's a strange creature whose pulse quickens at the sight of a fungus. Hunched and creeping over the old overgrown road, I must look strange indeed to my son who seems content to watch sunlight-loosened beads of dew slide down blades of grass. I must look stranger yet to the eyes of the woods—the deer we don't see but that certainly see us, the pair of red-tails casting their shadows intermittently alongside ours: a two-legged with a smaller two-legged by his side, bowing now and then to gather something from the leaf-rot.

For a week now the weather—hot spell after hard rains—has had me thinking mushrooms, and almost daily I've been bringing Luka into the woods in search of the mother lode we haven't quite found yet. To date we've picked a few baseball caps full. Mostly I pinch off the hollow stems and place the moist morels where the boy can find them, so that I can hear him say "and a mushroom!" but he's also found a few on his own, surprising me with his keen eye.

We're not looking for the Aunt-Edna-lode, though; we're searching for the gnome's stash, the Shangri-La from which we can fill a double-layered paper grocery sack as quick as we can pick. I've gotten gluttonous, I know, but I can taste the sliced caps cooked down in butter, salt, and pepper and piled atop a jack-cheese omelet. I'm thinking: mushroom reduction over elk backstrap. I'm thinking: stuff the trophy 'shrooms with poached Oregon salmon and fry them, ever so lightly, tempura-style.

I'd like to give a few bowlfuls, too, to our eighty-two-year-old neighbor, Frank, who, before his knees went bad, loved to hunt the hard-to-find fungi. Most of all, I'd like to harvest a few extra pounds to trade with the best chef in town for two meals at his bistro—to which I would take the well-deserving mother of my picking partner on a date I couldn't otherwise afford.

"Where are we?" Luka asks.

By now we're deep in the old burn, stooped over stumps whose charred bark flakes off in scales—the morels are everywhere, thickest in the thickest nettle patches. I cut farther in, not answering the boy I hold on my hip, bending over at every other step to pull morels from the pithy soil. Not worrying what effect these inane, imbalanced calisthenics will have on my hernia; not pausing to smell each fruit's damp, nutty scent, or to break a piece of burnt bark from a tree and mark our faces with it; not stopping to look at the scratches the whipping, thorny branches are leaving on Luka's arms and legs.

The ground blurs: a Monet of thistles, grass, and crumbling tree trunks. I can tell from the rhythm of my twig-cracking steps that I'm moving too fast. I backtrack, stare at the ground again: old stumps of 'shrooms I just picked. Seemingly everywhere a moment ago, the morels have disappeared, slunk back into the ground. Could I get any farther ahead of myself? Could I move any more hurriedly after these fruits of mulch and fire that do not move? Often while prepping for a meal, I'll slice open a cap and find along its inner walls a slug. *Slug always finds his 'shroom*, an oldtimer once told me. Slow down: move at Luka-pace. He's stumbling through the brambles with his lips pressed together, pushing a motorlike sound from his mouth, trying to imitate, I assume, the racket-causing, maple-boring pileated woodpecker that startled him a few moments ago. May light, soft as the underside of a leaf, falls on his face, on his head, which must be warm. *Go on, Great White Mushroom Hunter, run your fingers through the dark mat of his hair and feel the sun collecting there, press your nose to his scalp and smell spring arriving.*

Kana: a word or figure the Japanese haiku poets used as a kind of wonder-indicating syllable (it translates loosely into English as an exclamation point). Poet and haiku translator Robert Hass calls it "grammatical intensification." That heart-stutter we receive when an image of the world takes root in us: that's kana. A salient snap in time that arrests the senses or emotions enough to sear itself on the mind's otherwise distracted, refractive surface. Something to which our awareness has just been tuned—a small, stick-colored fungus that appears (*there, look down, next to your boot*), and becomes metaphoric of anything desired or worked for and simultaneously right before our eyes.

A winter ago I drove my then horse-obsessed son to our friends' small spread in the Bitterroot Valley so that he could see and perhaps feed a live horse. The whole drive up, he studied drawings of horses in books and pointed out the window at the pastured roans in snowy fields, saying, "Nay-nay, Nay-nay." When we reached the ranch, David brought out his daughters' toy horses and Luka galloped them around the close-cropped carpet meadow, looking over now and then to remind us of the equine presence: "Nay-nay, Nay-nay." But when we walked outside to the stall and Rose, a large chestnut mare, cantered up to the fence to greet us, I felt realization shiver through the body I carried. The big horse, nostrils dilated with curiosity, long face cocked inquisitively, stared the boy down. Luka gazed for a long while into the glossy brown eye that harbored his reflection, then turned to look at David and me, and decreed: "*Nay*-nay. *Nay*-nay." Now *that's* a horse.

Seventeenth-century haiku master Basho would've rendered that anecdote in a three-line poem, perhaps something like—

> *Small boy*
> *made smaller*
> *in the horse's eye.*

—but more precise, of course, more resonant. Because the haiku is wedded to "the instant" and to speed of comprehension, it serves as an ideal poetic net for the mind hoping to capture such minnow-quick moments of bafflement or awe. And because a good haiku mirrors the swiftness of the world it describes, the result is often a paradoxical slowing down that allows poet and reader alike to meditate on a single intrepid moment. Picking morels today with one eye on the ground and one eye on Luka, I keep thinking that the haiku poets, with their uncanny sense of detail—*Beads of dew / on the caterpillar's / hair*, wrote Buson—would have made amazing morel hunters. But Issa, who was enamored of children, chides my task-oriented brain in the face of Luka's goallessness:

> *The moon and the flowers—*
> *forty-nine years,*
> *walking around, wasting time.*

Better to keep my eyes tuned to my young Sherpa, spirit compass:

> *Closer to levitating*
> *than any monk—*
> *boy gazing at hovering hawk.*

Some days the double-layered paper grocery bag that is the heart, or the heart's memory, brims over with images such as these: moments of kana at Luka's kana, his amazement at the everyday (*use the commonplace to escape the commonplace*, Buson wrote). And some days I can feel Luka's wonder spurring me into deeper relation with the world, despite the too easily found ironies and horrors that tend to knock my romantic impulse on its rump and cause me to retreat into a spiritual hesitancy. This morning, for instance, I can't stop wondering if the soil from which my beloved morels have grown is laced with the same mine-tailings—arsenic and lead—that have made the upper portion of our valley an EPA Superfund site: the irony of the organic meal that leaves toxic grins on the foraging family's lips. This line of thinking quickly gains a dangerous momentum.

Gripped by casual cynicism, I pull back, disengage. But the boy's moment-to-moment discoveries pull me back in, drag me, the way he's dragging behind him a newly found whitetail antler: *Come along, now.* Toppling the coveted morels ($35 per pound in Chicago markets!) as he goes, he is either in a daze of boredom or he is walking kana, penetrated each step by the world, not penetrating it. It's tempting to call this spirit naïveté, but it's not: it's wisdom we lose along the way. Polish poet and Holocaust survivor Czeslaw Milosz echoed this dichotomy when he wrote:

> *Pure beauty and benediction: You are all I gathered*
> *from a life that was bitter and confused,*
> *in which I learned about evil, my own and not my own.*
> *Wonder kept seizing me, and I recall only wonder.*

I know the world is dying from my eyes, and that my affection for the world contributes to its destruction. I know also that it is emotionally safer to lie estranged beneath the false warmth of cynicism's down comforter each morning rather than venture into the world with a posture of openness, ready to receive, to live, rather than simply emote. Yet here I am, for starters, walking atop centuries of dead cottonwood leaves, while overhead new buds, sticky to the touch, smell like this: a sweet long-steeped tea, the sweaty neck of a lover, an infant's head. Last night, after soothing a nightmare-stricken Luka, I fell asleep alone on the couch and dreamed

I was still holding his small frame to my chest: his heart-beats, beating into my heart, sent a raw blue wind pulsing through my dream-body—I awoke quickened, a layer of the infinitely layered veil blown away.

Now, just now, Luka scrambles out from underneath a deadfall he's been referring to as his cave and hands a brittle leaf to me: "And a mushroom!"

"Oh—thank you," I say, and place the leaf with what we've gathered: a heaping load of morels, a bright orange flicker feather, a few rocks, a fork-horn whitetail shed.

Midafternoon—sun high, birds loud, dewdrops hard to find—Luka's nap is calling. I zip the bulging paper bag inside my backpack so our cache won't spill when we wade the river channel again. We'll cross the river and still be here, our existence intensified through our attention to the particular moments we inhabit.

Where are we? What canopy of clouds and birdsong have I lived beneath?

(2008)

TEDDY MACKER

THE KINGDOM
OF GOD

A meditation

IN A FAMILIAR MUDRA, a downstretched right hand, the Buddha touches the earth. What is the meaning of this gesture?

Another day alive. Down at the field, in the afternoon's whitest heat, my friend snaps open a cucumber. "It's like drinking a glass of water," he says.

Robert Louis Stevenson is walking down a street in Pitlochry when he sees a man kicking a dog. He grabs the man by the arm, yanks him away. "What're you doing?" the man sputters. "That's my dog!" "That's not your dog," Stevenson replies. "That's God's dog."

There are, some scientists say, five thousand different types of fireflies.

You can see my baby's heartbeat in the soft spot of her skull.

America has more shopping malls, says the bumper sticker, than high schools.

Every eleven years another billion people.

The Buddha was born under a tree, attained enlightenment under a tree, and died under a tree. *Shakyamuni* translates to "Sage of the Oak Tree People." When Jesus was approaching Jericho, crowds gathered at the road, but Zacchaeus, short, could not see Him. So Zacchaeus climbed a sycamore. "Zacchaeus," Christ said, looking up into the branches, "I would like to stay at your house."

It is another day and the suffering of this world continues. A mother pig shitting in the chute. A woman dodging stones.

In the last two hundred years the United States has lost 50 percent of its wetlands, 90 percent of its old-growth forests in the Northwest, and 99 percent of its tallgrass prairies. Martin Rees, England's Astronomer Royal and professor at Cambridge, gives mankind fifty-fifty odds of making it to 2100. This world, says an old Sanskrit poet, was made long ago by good men with big hearts; some sustained it while others subdued it and gave it away as if it were straw.

The other night, through the closed door, I heard my wife singing "The Rose" to hush our baby. At first I was tickled by her wobbly voice and the maudlin quality of the scene—but, listening more, I soon found myself totally undefended. Who was this woman in the bathroom? Who was she?

May my conscience hurt me into grace.

May the bees of attention fill the clear comb of the present.

May my knees know wood.

In Russia, a friend tells me, there are young girls who carve
turnips into small coffins to bury flies. Hearing this calls to
mind other great Artists of Life: Henry David Thoreau scent-
ing his handkerchief with an apple spray, the bride stepping
through the jungle at night wearing an anklet of fireflies,
Ryokan drinking sake with the farmers till all their eyebrows
turn white with snow; calls to mind the pen and paper along
the sill of the outhouse, the portrait of the wife painted on the
inside of the medieval shield, and the woman who woke me
from a nap so many years ago, a nap on a summer day, fan-
ning my sleeping face with the front of her dress.

If I were to quit worrying about what others thought of me,
friends and family in particular, how much more time would
I have in my day to do a reverence, do right by this world?
"What is clarity of mind?" a monk asks a master. "If two thousand people call to you," he replies, "and you don't look back."

In the alms of this moment, the mother stillness of the barn.

In the alms of this moment, the humble scornless million
hands of water.

The moon has not yet risen, the bed is warm with my wife. No
obstacles in my heart, everything a frailboned kindness.

In the alms of this moment, the whirling quiet of a resting
thigh.

In the alms of this moment, the exactful mystery of a baby's pink curling toes.

With my little knowledge, I have known, a handful of times, the greater knowledge. Once it happened standing shin deep in the Big Sur River, cobbles clattering at my feet.

In the alms of this moment, red hairline deltas on a woman's closed eyes.

Live close to the bone, suggests Thoreau. Live a single-gourd life, says the Chinese poet. A trunk and two handbags, offers D. H. Lawrence, are more than enough. And Jesus? Don't even bring along your stave. Buddha? Buddha scavenged rags from the graves of executed convicts.

In the alms of this moment, the lilac underside of a trout.

It is Lu Yu who perhaps moves me the most, the spirit attuned to the local pleasure, the little here, the life undistracted, the wonder. In my favorite poem of his he tells us his garden might be small but still it has yellow and purple plums . . . "What it all is," another poet once wrote, "I know not, but with gratitude the tears fall."

In a familiar mudra, a downstretched right hand, the Buddha touches the earth. What could be the meaning of this gesture? Later he will exhort followers to cease travel during the rainy season to avoid stepping on worms.

The train passes and I notice my wife's little hoop earring on the windowsill.

Crippled with joy, I see my daughter's gummy smile.

Once I stood shin deep in the Big Sur River, cobbles clattering at my feet.

(2011)

GEORGIANA VALOYCE-SANCHEZ

BREATHING THE ANCESTORS

The mystery behind the sun illumines a spiritual homecoming

WE HAVE COME to bury our dead. It is still dark. The dirt road leading down to Abalone Cove is rutted, and we bounce and sway in our seats as the van slowly winds its way down to the rocky shore. The people waiting below in the mist are like apparitions of the Ancestors we have come to return to the ocean. It is low tide, but the ghost-gray waves breaking along the dark shore leap high and wild, churning earth, rocks, and shells in their wake. Christ has arrived before me, shaking salt water from his hair, walking among the men in the darkness. He has walked these shores before, thousands of years before the first Christian missionaries ever arrived here. It is an old covenant, reflecting the light of Kakunupmawa, Mystery Behind the Sun.

The ashes of the Ancestors are close by. I cannot see them, but I know they are here. Several weeks before, I went with other Native Americans from different tribal cultures to the Arco Refinery in Carson, California, to see the reburial of the sixty or more native people who have been found there.

We walked in silence among the skeletal remains, the anthropologist hired by Arco making sure that we noted the evidence of violence on skulls and limbs. We are not sure who the people were, though some Chumash artifacts were also found with the bodies. The Chumash are my father's people, caretakers for thousands of years of a vast area of this land we now call southern California. What we do know is that something terrible took place there.

We have been called to Abalone Grove by the Tongva/Gabrieleno people, the most likely descendents of the Ancestors. Because the remains of the Ancestors were found on acknowledged Tongva land, it is proper that the Tongva take responsibility for the reburial. The Tongva, particularly the Ti'at Society, have decided to cremate the remains and return the Ancestors to the ocean.

When the Catholic missionaries came to California, the Tongva people were given the name "Gabrieleno" for the Mission San Gabriel, just as my father's people were given the name "Barbarena" for the Mission Santa Barbara, our original names subjugated, lost, Diegeno, Luiseno, Gabrieleno, Ventureno, Barbareno, Purismeno, Obisbeno . . .

We are still veiled in darkness, but the ocean is silver-gray in Abalone Cove. Dawn is just beyond the cliffs. What is this sorrow I feel?

The night before my father died, I attended a women's sweat. The heat and steam inside the darkness of the sweat lodge seemed unbearable. I was in the womb of God, unable to be born. *Creator, mercy. Please help my father to have a good death.* I could not take the suffering one minute longer, until the woman next to me, in pain from sitting on the hard earth, asked me to rub her back. The next day, my father died with all his loved ones around him. A good death. Simple acts. And we are born.

I dance in a circle of new light. Dawn has come to Abalone Cove. We are holding hands, dancing in a circle, a Friendship Dance some tribal cultures call it. We pray and dance to the Sunrise Song, to the Water Song, to the Rock Song. Sunsplashed ocean, dark cliffs, shadows, rocky shore move past me as if I were standing still and they were dancing in the round. Circles, circles everywhere, from sun to galaxies, plants on the hillside, animals scurrying to their homes, ocean life, every living cell of our bodies, and seabirds flying overhead.

I cannot understand the words sung by the Western Shoshone elder, but I understand their meaning—it is a great unknowing and it fills me with light. We offer Tongva and Chumash songs, Ancestor Songs and Healing Songs, songs with ancient words and meanings that we have remembered and reclaimed. I know these old songs—I have sung them before at other ceremonies and I sing, respectful, serious. Inside, I am filled with joy, smiling.

The ashes of the Ancestors are carried to the beach in plastic bags by some of the Tongva people. Several small plastic bags from the crematorium, each containing the remains or partial remains of a person, are placed on the sand. I wonder if the mother holding her baby was cremated with her child.

My sister Susan and I are honored to be chosen to help prepare the Ancestors for their journey out to sea. We kneel on the beach and line two large boxes with cloth. My favorite sweat lodge towel is used to line one of the boxes. It is the same towel we draped over the steel bars of the rented hospital bed when my father was dying. A fine mist of ash rises as we empty the plastic bags. My sister and I glance at one another. "We are breathing the Ancestors," I say. "Yes," she says.

Chumash and Tongva men lift the *ti'at*, the traditional plank canoe of the Tongva so like our own *tomol*, carrying her to the ocean's edge on their shoulders. Her name is Mo'omat

'Ahiko, "Breath of the Ocean," and she is draped in a garland of sage. The boxes holding the Ancestors' ashes are covered in a beautiful purple cloth with black hibiscus blossoms printed on it. Susan has woven a wreath of sage for the Ancestors and it is placed on top.

The Tongva people carry the Ancestors' ashes to the tí'at, the rest of us walking in solemn procession behind them. Waves crash against the canoe, lifting her each time, tossing her against the rocks, and she reminds me of a wild mustang, straining to be free of the hands that try to hold her down. The captain enters the canoe and directs the people to place the boxes in the center of the tí'at. As always, the Ancestors are our ballast, the steadying point of our journey on Earth.

The paddlers and other men begin to push the tí'at farther into the ocean, and she is bucking and heaving on the waves as the paddlers climb in and begin to paddle. Their long blades lift high into the air, circling down into the ocean and up again, like kayak paddlers, only with longer, larger paddles. They are beautiful to watch, and we pray earnestly for them to break beyond the pounding waves. Several of our men are still in the ocean, helping to push the tí'at into deeper water, and for a moment I am afraid she will not break free. *Creator, mercy.*

My brother John, who has followed the tí'at into the ocean, begins to sing the Dolphin Calling Song, praying for help for the paddlers. It is an old prayer, an old story: our people walking across a rainbow bridge, some falling into the depths of the ocean, only to be saved, changed into dolphins by the compassion of Hutash, the Spirit of the Earth, and Kakunupmawa. "'Alok'oy! 'Alok'oy!" Dolphin! Dolphin! And the tí'at breaks free of the waves—*Mo'omat 'Ahiko* is out in the open sea, long oars rising and falling, and she is skimming over the water. We sing, we sing, and our tears mingle with our shouts of encouragement. Farewell, Ancestors! Goodbye! Welcome home.

The captain of the ti'at told us later that when the boxes containing the ashes of the Ancestors were lowered into the ocean they sank immediately, slowly descending into the depths. Bubbles, like a thousand little breaths, rose from below, whispering in some ancient language as they broke through the ocean's surface. I hear them sometimes.

I breathe the Ancestors and they breathe me. Because I breathe the Old Ones, because I love the Mystical Heart of Christianity, because I find goodness and truth in all the world's religions, I don't quite fit anywhere. I am an anomaly.

Sometimes, I am like the *Mo'omat 'Ahiko*, tossed between deep ocean and rocky shore. It is a difficult place to be, but I know this—God, Kakunupmawa, Mystery Behind the Sun, is good. Life with Hutash, the Spirit of the Earth, is good. I have been given teachers, ceremonies, stories, and songs; with the Ancestors, they are my ballast, my steadying point as I head out for the deep.

(2004)

JOHN CALDERAZZO

SAILING THROUGH THE NIGHT

"Thoughts which day turns into smoke and mist stand
about us in the night as light and flames; even as the
column which fluctuates above the crater of Vesuvius,
in the day time appears a pillar of cloud, but by night a
pillar of fire."
—*Henry David Thoreau, "Night and Moonlight"*

FOR MORE THAN TWENTY YEARS I've been thinking about a
few seconds of film. In a newsreel taken in Asia during the
Vietnam War, a saffron-robed monk sitting in a lotus posi-
tion allows himself to be doused with gasoline. Suddenly his
bright saffron robes explode into an even brighter orange, and
flames begin to climb his neck. Yet somehow he continues to
sit without moving or crying out, continues to meditate even
as the terrible fire shoots up the side of his face. Finally, he
crumples to the side, a human torch illuminating the unreal
horror and waste of war.

That film clip was a cultural and generational marker of
the late 1960s, and anyone who saw it is likely to see it again,

probably without wanting to, in the unruly theater of memory. The older I get, the more I am haunted by those flames.

Or I should say I am haunted by the monk himself, an anonymous and middle-aged man, maybe younger than I am now. Often these days I lie awake at night and listen to the wind roaring out of the mountains and over my comfortable Colorado home, wind that occasionally roars like fire, and I wonder what brought that man to make that decision.

I mean the man himself, as much as I can separate him from his monkish traditions of social responsibility and sacrifice. A mother's son full of bravery and fear and desire—had he lost hope in a world full of war? Or was he mostly affirming life, believing that his final act would engender other acts to stop violence? Or was he gripped by something completely beyond my understanding, an emotion or a way of thinking like an invisible color on the spectrum of human experience, a bright band of light shimmering in front of me that somehow I still haven't learned how to see?

Or maybe it's not the monk I am haunted by. Maybe it's me, my confusion about how to handle the seemingly endless bad news of the world. I have come to probably the halfway point in my life, a life blessed mainly with privilege and good fortune, yet more and more often I worry about how I'll get through the rest of it without giving in to cynicism or self-indulgence or despair. And until I learn to find some balance between action and acceptance, I suspect that I'll keep throttling myself with questions about suffering and heartbreak and the darker exhalations of the human soul.

I'm five years old, and I'm squatting on the sidewalk, watching black ants pour out of a crack in the cement. They're running everywhere—frantic, insane, incensed. At the urging of my friend Herb, I've just reached down with a stick and scrambled their hill.

"You know," says Herb, in his sly, older-boy voice, "ants don't sleep—not ever. And if you're not careful, they'll follow you home, just to get even."

That night I pull the covers over my head and scrunch my face into the pillow. The ants are coming—I can practically hear them marching down the sidewalk. Eventually they'll find our house, squeeze under the front door, file up the stairs, and climb the bed legs. They'll swarm into my nose and mouth, they'll gnaw my eyes. I lie awake in the heavy darkness, wondering if I should sneak downstairs and cram a towel under the door, or wake up my parents and little brother and confess to the catastrophe I've wrought, this wrathful army of insects bearing down on the house.

I wonder how often insomnia starts that way—not necessarily in a childhood in Dachau or Somalia or Bedford-Stuyvesant, but in some half-forgotten moment, an absurd pang of guilt that the routine cruelties of the world transform over the years into a firestorm of worry, into hours of working out the permutations of disaster, into an unwise but inevitable blurring of private and public dread.

Or maybe all of this is fueled by getting older. Or by a visit to a doctor—say, for a case of poison ivy. In my case the bubbly rashes were an amusing and slightly embarrassing affliction for an adult who should have known better, an outdoor guy who should have looked before wading into the backyard hedges to pull weeds. Amusing until the moment I felt the doctor's cold finger press into my back and heard him say, "What's this? This I don't like *at all*."

His finger pressed into a black spot the size of a quarter, a mole that somehow my wife SueEllen and I hadn't noticed. Melanoma, a surgeon soon confirmed over the telephone as I sat silent and alone in our kitchen one afternoon. Malignant.

Even after I had it cut out, along with a hand-size chunk of skin, the surgeon said that there was a chance, always a chance, that a rogue cell might have worked itself deeper in, so that sometimes even now, nine years after the surgery and with statistics piling up on my side, I lie awake wondering where that pinprick of darkness might have gone, that death star sailing through the infinity of my body.

We bomb Baghdad. On television, dream images of green, glowing rockets slide across the night. Then we invade. Even after I pull away from the set and try to walk off my anger, I hear the muffled shouts of hungry and abandoned Iraqi conscripts who've been buried alive in long trenches, tractored into the earth by the hundreds. The teenagers who helped do this to them look into the camera and say, as they've been told to say, "We got a job to do, and when we finish we'll be outta here."

I watch friends speak at peace rallies in town, and I think: I should join them up there, I'm articulate and not shy, I should write letters, I should make phone calls, I should march, I should fast. In 1989, with willpower alone, a skinny young man in China stopped a row of enormous tanks— didn't we all see this on television?

Then I think, What fools we are to keep yammering at each other, the naïve or the already-converted, or the philo-. sophically dispossessed, or the hard-up-for-thrills-of-the-Sixties. In China, those tanks rumbled through Tiananmen Square anyway. The damage in Iraq and Kuwait has already been done. And besides, Sadam's a killer and a sociopath, even if our main interest in suddenly getting rid of him is fueled by oil, not justice.

A woman I know and like takes the microphone and starts waving her arms, as though she really thinks she can redirect the gales of history. Where does her optimism come from?

More than twenty years ago, an Asian monk decided to die an awful death, and a year later, a boy I knew in high school, a star hurdler, lost his legs in the Vietnam highlands. The war went on forever.

The woman at the microphone talks and talks. I rock on my heels, my fists jammed in my pockets. Then I wander off to find a beer.

For three nights now, winds have boomed like surf against the bedroom wall. They rattle the double storm windows next to my head. Fifty miles an hour, sixty, seventy—they plunge from the high country through narrow canyons into our moonlit valley, the meeting point of mountains and plains. No matter how many pillows I burrow under, I can hear our big cottonwoods creaking and cracking, waving their limbs like dervishes.

I'm desperate for sleep, desperate not to wake SueEllen. Last night, after hours of being elbowed and kicked, she pulled me close and whispered, "Those elk we saw last week when we walked in the meadow—remember? How still they sat with the sun on their backs, and wildflowers everywhere, Queen Anne's lace, Indian paintbrush, mountain bluebells...."

SueEllen's night mantras: meditations on loveliness, haiku just for me. Often they help. But not last night. Or tonight—the gusts roar in from some far corner of the universe, and our big blue spruce shudders and lashes the window behind my head. It's a tree the previous owners planted after the neighbor's picnic table, lifted by the wind, came flying through the glass.

I close my eyes and try to think of good things—my marriage and job, deep friendships, our small cheerful nieces— but suddenly I'm staring at the ceiling, then out through the backyard window and up into the blades of our windmill. On calm nights the windmill stands against the stars like a giant silver daisy shining in moonlight. But tonight the blades are flying. They blur and turn into a propeller, a murderous flower whirring, whirring.

A squall starts whining in my skull, prying loose nightmares, ragged clots of thought: Amazon forests bulldozed to extinction, a midnight call—aren't they always at midnight?—saying a friend has died in a car wreck, a monk sitting in robes of fire.

This is the time of night when anything can come sailing through the window, when one thought multiplies to infinity. This is the time of night when tumors grow.

"Oh, John...," sighs SueEllen, twisting away from me to salvage what she can of her sleep. So I throw an arm over her and watch elk drift through green mountains, feel my cross-country skis glide over diamond fields of snow.

I think of Zach, the son of good friends. One afternoon when he was about two, he and I, out walking, found a golden aspen leaf on the wet sidewalk. "Look," I said, peeling it off the concrete, holding it up by the stem so he could watch sunlight stream through it. Then I let it go. The leaf butterflied down, danced and flipped in the sunlight. When it landed, Zach jumped with delight, his eyes huge, his blonde curls flying. You'd think it had fallen from the only tree on earth.

"Again!" he said.

I picked it up and let it drop.

"Again!"

By his fourth request I was bored. But by the sixth or seventh something had begun to happen. As I watched Zach lasering in, I found myself slipping into his way of seeing things. And finally, like a small boy, I saw something astounding: a golden leaf falling out of the sky.

Sometimes, when sleepless nights come in binges, I find myself preparing for the night during the day. I work hard at my teaching job, which I love, and then make sure to exhaust myself by riding my bike miles up the canyons or around and around our valley. I skip the television news, cancel the newspaper, cut back on coffee. For a year, I drink nothing alcoholic.

Or: Sitting cross-legged in front of the television, I sip Jim Beam while a psychologist says that long-time pessimists develop more chronic diseases than optimists do. It doesn't help that I write magazine articles and essays about the forests of Thailand shaved clean of elephants and tigers, or read about a computer that will simulate the constellations fifty years from now, when filth in our own atmosphere will keep us from actually seeing the stars.

Even as I write, even as I jet off somewhere to tramp through a jungle that seems always to have shrunk down to a green dot, even as I scribble in my reporter's notebook in the glare of the malignant sun, whose greasy light I keep trying to scrape off my arms, I realize that I've grown slightly ill. At night the fever only rises.

And so I've come to California to learn how to wash dishes. With maybe a hundred others, environmental activists mostly, I'm listening to Thich Nhat Hanh, a Vietnamese monk and teacher who is sitting cross-legged on a low stage. He's flanked by flower vases and wisps of burning incense. His brown robes hang motionless from his thin frame.

"We need to be mindful of the present moment," he says slowly. "We need to be aware of what is happening to us right now. For example, if I am washing the dishes, I should pay full attention to the dishes. If I rush through them just to be done, or if I keep thinking about the tea I will drink when I'm finished, then I'm not capable of being fully alive during the time I'm washing the dishes."

I close my eyes and see big-eyed Zach staring at the wet

sidewalk. A golden leaf blots out the blue sky.

I open my eyes and see Thich Nhat Hanh smiling at me. It's an exceptionally intelligent smile that radiates inward *and* outward, a practiced Buddha smile that nevertheless looks as guileless as a glass of water. It comforts me in this room full of people I don't entirely trust, this room near Los Angeles with too many men my age wearing ponytails and more women in serapes than I've seen in years. The place is festering with goodwill, and I keep expecting somebody to break out a guitar.

But I suspect that one of the people I don't entirely trust is *me*, me with all my knee-jerk biases. There are damn good people here, I tell myself, pragmatic and tough-minded visionaries, a lot of them, who just need some rest from years of seventy-hour work weeks. Still, I can't shake the notion that I'm sitting inside a colossal cliché. "The Sound of One Lung Coughing"—that's what I'd call the story I could write about this week. On the other hand, meditation is one of the most difficult things I've ever tried, a slippery slope I can't seem to hang on to, and I don't know if I'm strong enough to make it through the week.

Here I am, though, sitting cross-legged on a cushion like everyone else, my knees aching.

I try smiling back at Thich Nhat Hanh, but I feel stiff. He looks as unwrinkled as a teenager, yet he's at least in his mid-sixties. Chairman of the Vietnamese Buddhist Peace Delegation during the Vietnam War, exiled from his homeland for his war resistance, he was nominated by Martin Luther King, Jr. for the Nobel Peace Prize and has worked with war refugees for twenty-five years. Somehow he's found a balance between action and acceptance, a way to neither retreat from the world's suffering nor let it burn him up from the inside.

"If I am chewing a string bean," he tells us, "I should

be mindful of the string bean. I should give it my full attention so it will reveal its true nature to me. If I am chewing
the string bean and thinking of baseball, then I'm chewing...
baseball!"

I laugh with everyone else. Thich Nhat Hanh's laughing,
too. A thousand tiny muscles in my face begin to let go. Later,
when I close my eyes and try to meditate, I can feel the room
fill up with breathing, a great orange glow.

The Serbs bomb the Croats. Hunger bombs Africa. Another
window-rattling, sheet-twisting night, the windmill flying. The
full moon burns my face with a lunar tan, blue and dangerous.

I hear a long rumble, or maybe I make it up. It comes
from the Bellvue Dome, a spectacular rock formation shaped
like a giant ramp that walls in part of our valley. Its red cliffs
face our house; the ramp slopes off to the east and the Great
Plains. The Dome is the first foothill of the Rockies, the first
great rise in two thousand miles, and not that long ago it was
used by the Arapaho to kill bison.

I hear them now, animals rumbling up from the plains.
Heads down, they charge into a wind they barely notice
because leather-clad hunters are yelling and flapping animal
skins to funnel them uphill. Their eyes swivel with fear.

Now they're galloping over the edge, shaking the earth.
They snort and scream, paw and stamp the air. A river of fur
pours over the cliffs. The wind blows out of the mountains
over miles of bison, a continent of animals surging toward the
cliffs under enormous dust clouds. Behind it all, dimly visible,
come lines of covered wagons, then railroads, steam engines
puffing west.

The wind rises, and somehow I realize that I can control
it, whip it into a hurricane. So I do: I make it blow up until it
stops the bison in mid-fall, then pushes them back over the

Dome and back out onto the grasslands, which are tossing and rolling, rolling. The wind slashes the wagon covers, lifts the wagons and flings them back over the horizon. It rips up the iron tracks and the trains. Yes, I tell myself as I lie in bed smiling at the ceiling, the tracks are flying up from the ground, and now I'm sending the wind over the earth's curve and through an arc of time, I'm sending it to Asia, where it blows out a wooden match that is poised to make a man in robes turn into fire....

This is my ghost dance, a desperate act of imagining that annihilates the past and edits the future. Like the plains Indians of the 1890s who were cornered into dreaming back a lost continent full of animals, I cling to this vision.

But I'm beginning to wonder if I'm just chewing baseball. Dancing back and forth through history and stopping anywhere but here—right here in the present moment—didn't work for the Sioux, so why should it work for me? The moon is beating down and SueEllen is breathing beside me. The time is *always* right now. Why can't I let the wind just be wind and not the stirrings of the apocalypse?

"Give me silence, water, hope," writes the great poet Pablo Neruda. "Give me struggle, iron, volcanoes." After puzzling over those lines for years, I think I'm starting to see what he means. I'm writing a book about volcanoes, maybe an odd topic for an English professor. But volcanoes, I'm beginning to think, are incendiary with hope.

I fly to Italy and climb Vesuvius, which smothered Pompeii. I sit on the broken and burnt-red rim of its crater and watch steam hiss from small cracks. In Sicily, I drive a car around the base of Etna and buy tomatoes from an old woman sitting in a field, its soil rich from centuries of nourishing ash. She looks like my father's mother, who died years ago. Over her shoulder, the volcano rolls with smoke, hard black lava rivers stretching for miles. Thousand-year-old towns and vine-yards sit on lava slopes that once simmered and welled like tar a hundred miles below the earth's surface. The woman smiles at me and the tomatoes explode in my mouth.

On the island volcano of Stromboli, I walk along black pebbled beaches that shine like sealskin. Fishermen drag their boats from the water, and every ten or fifteen minutes I hear what sounds like a dragon exhaling. Faces turn to the sky. It's the mountain erupting, the earth breathing fire and putting out new earth—the newest anywhere. At night, in a boat bob-bing offshore, I watch orange lava splatter from its summit.

I begin to *feel*, not just understand, how winds can move under the ground. I don't mean Colorado mountain squalls or even the fiery gusts that Aristotle and Pliny the Elder thought blew through the center of the world, causing earthquakes. I mean centuries and centuries of rock wind, siroccos of iron and granite, glowing lava zephyrs, stone currents. And moun-tain ranges and continents that have been bulging up and wearing down for more than four billion years.

I'm finding solace in the liquid nature of rock, in the im-permanent nature of everything.

Give me volcanoes, iron, hope.

Back home one afternoon, I hike in a river basin full of chang-ing aspens. A cloud sliding over a far ridge reminds me of the glacier that once carved out the valley. I stand very still, just breathing. I inhale, and down slides the glacier, a long white tongue that soon fills up my view. I exhale. The ice pulls back, leaving a valley full of newly minted elk and flowers. Miles below me, deep in the earth, I can practically hear the grinding of con-tinental plates coming together and tearing apart. Yes, it's good to know that North America has been a drifter, a pilgrim, too.

My eyes are opening to time in fast-forward and reverse, atoms that swirl through dreams and disappointments, a man's flesh turned to fire to blowing ashes to tough new grass, a house-sized boulder rearranging itself through millennia as surely as a cloud. Is this kind of world-breath a kind of optimism? I begin to see it even when I stand in my shower at home, the shiny plastic curtain a world map whose green and orange continents buckle with an offhand sweep of my arm, whose once-unclimbable mountains crumple or flatten out in my soapy hands.

A volcanologist I know tells me that even the planet's crust bulges out under the moon's pull. The universe breathes; everything sails along in its wind: rattling windows, rogue cells, bison, rainforest, bombs, eruptions of hatred and peace and goodwill.

I need to remember to remember this.

One summer morning after a passable night's sleep, I get up, shower, and sit on the edge of our patio, my bare feet on the grass. I'm clipping my toenails. After a while, I notice something moving near my feet. It's one of my toenails—upright, luminous as a sliver of moon—and it seems to be wandering off, as though it's decided to walk to Kansas. It bumps slowly along through the shadowy grass. I lean forward, bend down. It takes me a while to find the ant struggling underneath it, half its size. The tiny legs work furiously.

A second later I see my own death.

I don't mean a cold finger in the back or even the dying itself. I mean the steady fires of decay and regrowth, the redistribution of myself—light, heat, bones, hair, heart—into the great wide windy world. "If only I could be like the tree at the river's edge, every year turning green again," says the Cold Mountain poet of China. I used to wish for that, too, of course, and most of the time I still do. But then I remind myself that even a redwood breaks through the earth as a redwood for only a moment or so before falling back into the immensity of time.

I sit on the patio and watch my toenail walk away. I smile. I almost wave.

(1995)

ANTHONY DOERR

WINDOW OF
POSSIBILITY

Why the Hubble Ultra Deep Field is the most
incredible photograph ever taken

WE LIVE ON EARTH. Earth is a clump of iron and magne-
sium and nickel, smeared with a thin layer of organic matter,
and sleeved in vapor. It whirls along in a nearly circular orbit
around a minor star we call the sun.

I know, the sun doesn't *seem* minor. The sun puts the
energy in our salads, milkshakes, hamburgers, gas tanks, and
oceans. It literally makes the world go round. And it's huge:
The Earth is a chickpea and the sun is a beach ball. The sun
comprises 99.9 percent of all the mass in the solar system.
Which means Earth, Mars, Jupiter, Saturn, etc., all fit into that
little 0.1 percent.

But, truly, our sun is exceedingly minor. Almost incom-
prehensibly minor.

We call our galaxy the Milky Way. There are at least 100
billion stars in it and our sun is one of those. A hundred billion is a big number, and humans are not evolved to appreci-
ate numbers like that, but here's a try: If you had a bucket

with a thousand marbles in it, you would need to procure 999,999 more of those buckets to get a billion marbles. Then you'd have to repeat the process a hundred times to get as many marbles as there are stars in our galaxy.

That's a lot of marbles.

So. The Earth is massive enough to hold all of our cities and oceans and creatures in the sway of its gravity. And the sun is massive enough to hold the Earth in the sway of its gravity. But the sun itself is merely a mote in the sway of the gravity of the Milky Way, at the center of which is a vast, concentrated bar of stars, around which the sun swings (carrying along Earth, Mars, Jupiter, Saturn, etc.) every 230 million years or so. Our sun isn't anywhere near the center; it's way out on one of the galaxy's minor arms. We live beyond the suburbs of the Milky Way. We live in Nowheresville.

But still, we are in the Milky Way. And that's a big deal, right? The Milky Way is at least a major *galaxy*, right?

Not really. Spiral-shaped, toothpick-shaped, sombrero-shaped—in the visible universe, at any given moment, there are hundreds of thousands of millions of galaxies. Maybe as many as 125 billion. There very well may be more galaxies in the universe than there are stars in the Milky Way.

So. Let's say there are 100 billion stars in our galaxy. And let's say there are 100 billion galaxies in our universe. At any given moment, then, assuming ultra-massive and dwarf galaxies average each other out, there might be 10,000,000,000,000,000,000,000 stars in the universe. That's 1.0×10^{22}. That's 10 sextillion.

Here's a way of looking at it: there are enough stars in the universe that if everybody on Earth were charged with naming his or her share, we'd each get to name a trillion and a half of them.

Even that number is still impossibly hard to comprehend—if you named a star every time your heart beat for your whole life, you'd have to live about 375 lifetimes to name your share.

Last year, a handful of astronomers met in London to vote on the top ten images taken by the Hubble Telescope in its sixteen years in operation. They chose some beauties: the Cat's Eye Nebula, the Sombrero Galaxy, the Hourglass Nebula. But conspicuously missing from their list was the Hubble Ultra Deep Field image. It is, I believe, the most incredible photograph ever taken.

In 2003, Hubble astronomers chose a random wedge of sky just below the constellation Orion and, during four hundred orbits of the Earth, over the course of several months, took a photograph with a million-second-long exposure. It was something like peering through an eight-foot soda straw with one big, superhuman eye at the same wedge of space for eleven straight nights.

What they found there was breathtaking: a shard of the early universe that contains a bewildering array of galaxies and pre-galactic lumps. Scrolling through it is eerily similar to peering at a drop of pond water through a microscope: one expects the galaxies to start squirming like paramecia. It bewilders and disorients; the dark patches swarm with questions. If you peered into just one of its black corners, took an Ultra Deep Field of the Ultra Deep Field, would you see as much all over again?

What the Ultra Deep Field image ultimately offers is a singular glimpse at ourselves. Like Copernicus's *On the Revolutions of the Celestial Spheres*, it resets our understanding of who and what we are.

As of early April 2007, astronomers had found 204 planets outside our solar system. They seem to be everywhere we look. Chances are, many, many stars have planets or systems of planets swinging around them. What if *most* suns have solar systems? If our sun is one in 10 sextillion, could our Earth be one in 10 sextillion as well? Or the Earth might be one— just *one*, the only one, *the* one. Either way, the circumstances are mind-boggling.

The Hubble Ultra Deep Field is an infinitesimally slender core-sample drilled out of the universe. And yet inside it is enough vastness to do violence to a person's common sense. How can the window of possibility be so unfathomably large?

Take yourself out to a field some evening after everyone else is asleep. Listen to the migrant birds whisking past in the dark; listen to the creaking and settling of the world. Think about the teeming, microscopic worlds beneath your shoes—the continents of soil, the galaxies of bacteria. Then lift your face up.

The night sky is the coolest Advent calendar imaginable: it is composed of an infinite number of doors. Open one and find ten thousand galaxies hiding behind it, streaming away at hundreds of miles per second. Open another, and another. You gaze up into history; you stare into the limits of your own understanding. The past flies toward you at the speed of light. Why are you here? Why are the stars there? Is it even remotely possible that our one, tiny, eggshell world is the only one encrusted with life?

The Hubble Ultra Deep Field image should be in every classroom in the world. It should be on the president's desk. It should probably be in every church, too.

"To sense that behind anything that can be experienced," Einstein once said, "there is a something that our mind cannot grasp and whose beauty and sublimity reaches us only indirectly and as a feeble reflection, this is religiousness."

Whatever we believe in—God, children, nationhood—
nothing can be more important than to take a moment every
now and then and accept the invitation of the sky: to leave the
confines of ourselves and fly off into the hugeness of the universe, to disappear into the inexplicable, the implacable, the
reflection of that something our minds cannot grasp.

(2007)

CONTRIBUTORS

Poet, essayist, and naturalist **Diane Ackerman** is the author of two dozen highly acclaimed works of nonfiction and poetry, including *A Natural History of the Senses* and *The Zookeeper's Wife*, winner of the Orion Book Award. She has received a Guggenheim Fellowship, the John Burroughs Award, and the Lavan Poetry Prize, and been honored as a Literary Lion by the New York Public Library. Her piece in this anthology is an excerpt from *Dawn Light*, published by W. W. Norton; it is used by permission.

Susanne Antonetta's most recent book, *Inventing Family*, a memoir and study of adoption, is forthcoming from W. W. Norton. Awards for her poetry and prose include a New York Times Notable Book, an American Book Award, a Library Journal Best Science Book of the Year, a Lenore Marshall Award finalist, a Pushcart prize, and others. She is also coauthor of *Tell It Slant: Creating, Refining, and Publishing Creative Nonfiction*. Her essays and poems have appeared in the *New York Times*, the *Washington Post, Seneca Review*, and many anthologies. She lives in Bellingham, Washington, with her husband and son.

Rick Bass, an American writer and environmental activist, is the author of many books, including *The Wild Marsh, Why I Came West*, and *The Lives of Rocks*. Several of his books have been finalists for the National Book Critics Circle Award and the Los Angeles Times Book Award, as well as the New York Times and Los Angeles Times Best Book of the Year. He's been awarded fellowships from the National Endowment for the Arts and the Guggenheim Foundation, and his short stories and essays have received O. Henry and Pushcart Prizes and been widely anthologized. He lives and works in the Yaak Valley in Montana.

Michael P. Branch is a professor of literature and environment at the University of Nevada, Reno. He has published many books and articles on environmental literature, and his creative nonfiction has appeared in *Utne Reader, Ecotone, Hawk and Handsaw,* and many other magazines. His blog series, "Rants from the Hill," appears monthly in *High Country News* online. Mike lives with his wife and two daughters at six thousand feet in the western Nevada desert, where the Great Basin and the Sierra Nevada meet.

John Calderazzo's work has appeared in *Audubon, Georgia Review, High Country News, North American Review,* and *Witness,* among other places. His work has been cited in *Best American Stories* and *Best American Essays,* and has appeared in *American Nature Writing* and *Best Adventure Travel Stories.* His most recent book is *Rising Fire: Volcanoes & Our Inner Lives.* He teaches nonfiction writing at Colorado State University, where he cofounded an interdisciplinary climate change education and outreach program.

Anthony Doerr lives in Boise, Idaho. He is the author of four books: *Memory Wall, The Shell Collector, About Grace,* and *Four Seasons in Rome,* and his writing has won The Story Prize, two Pushcart prizes, the Rome Prize, the New York Public Library's Young Lions Award, the Barnes & Noble Discover Prize, a Guggenheim Fellowship, and four O. Henry Prizes.

Chris Dombrowski's books include the chapbook *Fragments with Dusk in Them* and the poetry collection *By Cold Water*. His second collection of poems, *Earth Again*, is forthcoming in spring 2013 from Wayne State University Press. He has been a river guide in Montana for sixteen summers.

Brian Doyle is the editor of *Portland Magazine* at the University of Portland, and the author most recently of a novella, *Cat's Foot*. His greatest ambition is total honking humility, which he believes will lead to final total perception of the inundation of wonder at which he will gape open-mouthed and drooling just like his kids used to, in rivers and torrents, so much so that he had to attach little tin buckets to their shirts. Those were great days. He still has the buckets.

David Gessner is the author of eight books, including *My Green Manifesto* and *The Tarball Chronicles*. He has published essays in many magazines, including *The New York Times Magazine*, and won the John Burroughs Award for his *Orion* piece "Learning to Surf." He taught environmental writing as a Briggs-Copeland Lecturer at Harvard, and is currently a professor at the University of North Carolina at Wilmington, where he founded the award-winning literary journal of place, *Ecotone*.

Aleria Jensen is a fourth-generation Alaskan who works as a marine conservation biologist in Juneau. Her writing has appeared in the *Potomac Review* and the *Alaska Quarterly Review*.

Teddy Macker, husband, father, gardener, and poet, lives in the Painted Cave community in the Santa Ynez Mountains of California. His work appears in the *Antioch Review*, *Poetry East*, *The Massachusetts Review*, *The Sun*, and elsewhere.

Amy Leach is the author of the essay collection *Things That Are*. She holds an MFA in creative nonfiction from the University of Iowa, and her work has appeared in *Best American Essays, A Public Space, Orion*, and *The Gettysburg Review*, among other journals. She has been recognized with the Whiting Writers' Award and a Rona Jaffe Foundation Award and lives in Montana.

Scott Russell Sanders lives in the hardwood hill country of southern Indiana. Among his more than twenty books are novels, collections of stories, and works of personal nonfiction, including *Hunting for Hope, A Private History of Awe*, and *A Conservationist Manifesto*. His most recent book is *Earth Works: Selected Essays*. He is a Distinguished Professor Emeritus of English at Indiana University.

Georgiana Valoyce-Sanchez has been an American Indian Studies lecturer at California State University, Long Beach, since 1986. Several of her poems have appeared in the anthology *The Sound of Rattles and Clappers*, and her essay "Breathing the Ancestors" appeared in *Face to Face: Women Writers on Faith, Mysticism and Awakening*.

Ann Zwinger is the author of numerous books, including the acclaimed *Run, River, Run; Wind in the Rock; Downcanyon; The Near-Sighted Naturalist*; and, most recently, *Shaped by Wind and Water: Reflections of a Naturalist*. She lives in Colorado Springs.

ABOUT ORION MAGAZINE

SINCE 1982, *Orion* has been a meeting place for people who seek a conversation about nature and culture that is rooted in beauty, imagination, and hope. Through the written word, the visual arts, and the ideas of our culture's most imaginative thinkers, *Orion* seeks to craft a vision for a better future for both people and planet.

Reader-supported and totally advertising-free, *Orion* blends scientific thinking with the arts, and the intellectual with the emotional. *Orion* has a long history of publishing the work of established writers from Wendell Berry, Terry Tempest Williams, and Barry Lopez to Rebecca Solnit, Luis Alberto Urrea, and Sandra Steingraber.

Orion is also grounded in the visual arts, publishing picture essays and art portfolios that challenge the traditional definition of "environment" and invite readers to think deeply about their place in the natural world. *Orion*'s website, www.orionmagazine.org, features multimedia web extras including slide shows and author interviews, as well as opportunities for readers to discuss *Orion* articles.

Orion is published bimonthly by The Orion Society, a nonprofit 501(c)3 organization, and is available in both print and digital editions.

Subscribe

Orion publishes six beautiful, inspiring issues per year. To get a free trial issue, purchase a subscription, or order a gift subscription, please visit www.orionmagazine.org/subscribe or call 888/254-3713.

Support

Orion depends entirely on the generous support of readers and foundations to publish the magazine and books like this one. To support *Orion*, please visit www.orionmagazine.org/donate, or send a contribution directly to *Orion* at 187 Main Street, Great Barrington, MA, 01230.

To discuss making a gift of stock or securities, or for information about how to include *Orion* in your estate plans, please call us at 888/254-3713, or send an e-mail to development@orionmagazine.org.

Shop

Head to the *Orion* website, www.orionmagazine.org, to purchase *Orion* books, organic cotton t-shirts, and other merchandise featuring the distinctive *Orion* logo. Back issues from the past thirty years are also available.

MORE BOOKS FROM ORION

ORION READERS

Orion Readers collect landmark *Orion* essays into short thematic volumes:

Change Everything Now. A selection of essays about ecological urgency.

Thirty-Year Plan: Thirty Writers on What We Need to Build a Better Future. An eloquent statement on the future of humanity.

Wonder and Other Survival Skills. A collection of thoughtful and inspirational writing on our relationship to the natural world.

Beyond Ecophobia: Reclaiming the Heart in Nature Education, by David Sobel. An expanded version of one of *Orion*'s most popular articles that speaks to those interested in nurturing in children the ability to understand and care deeply for nature from an early age.

Into the Field: A Guide to Locally Focused Learning, by Claire Walker Leslie, John Tallmadge, and Tom Wessels, with an introduction by Ann Zwinger. Curriculum ideas for teachers interested in taking their students out of doors.

Place-Based Education: Connecting Classrooms & Communities, by David Sobel. A guide for using the local community and environment as the starting place for curriculum learning, strengthening community bonds, appreciation for the natural world, and a commitment to citizen engagement.

ORION ANTHOLOGIES

Finding Home: Writing on Nature and Culture from Orion *Magazine,* edited by Peter Sauer. An anthology of the best writing from *Orion* published from 1982 to 1992.

The Future of Nature: Writing on a Human Ecology from Orion *Magazine,* selected and introduced by Barry Lopez. An anthology of the best writing from *Orion* published from 1992 to 2007.

FOR EDUCATORS

Ideal for reading groups and academic course adoption, many *Orion* books are accompanied by a downloadable teacher's guide consisting of key discussion questions. Teacher's guides can be found on the *Orion* website at www.orionmagazine .org/education.

Series design by Hans Teensma,
principal of the design studio Impress
(www.impressinc.com), which has
designed *Orion* since 1998.
The typeface is Scala, designed by Dutch
typographer Martin Majoor in 1990.
Printed by BookMobile.